ANTI-RACISM

Anti-racism has without doubt become a powerful component of modern society but, unlike its counter-discourses of racism and ethnic hatred, has remained curiously inconspicuous as a subject of social and historical analysis. This introductory text provides students for the first time with a historical and international analysis of the development of anti-racism. Drawing on sources from around the world, the author explains the roots and describes the practice of anti-racism in Western and non-Western societies from Britain and the United States to Malaysia and Brazil.

Topics covered include:

- the historical roots of anti-racism
- the relationship between nationalism, capitalism and anti-racism
- the practice of anti-racism
- the theoretical and political dilemmas of anti-racism
- the politics of backlash

This lively, concise book will be an indispensable resource for all students interested in issues of 'race' and ethnicity and in contemporary society more generally.

Alastair Bonnett is Lecturer in Geography at the University of Newcastle upon Tyne.

KEY IDEAS

SERIES EDITOR: PETER HAMILTON, THE OPEN UNIVERSITY, MILTON KEYNES

Designed to complement the successful *Key Sociologists*, this series covers the main concepts, issues, debates, and controversies in sociology and the social sciences. The series aims to provide authoritative essays on central topics of social science, such as community, power, work, sexuality, inequality, benefits and ideology, class, family, etc. Books adopt a strong individual 'line' constituting original essays rather than literary surveys, and form lively and original treatments of their subject matter. The books will be useful to students and teachers of sociology, political science, economics, psychology, philosophy, and geography.

Class
STEPHEN EDGELL

Consumption
ROBERT BOCOCK

Culture
CHRIS JENKS

Globalization
MALCOLM WATERS

Lifestyle
DAVID CHANEY

Mass Media
PIERRE SORLIN

Moral Panics
KENNETH THOMPSON

Postmodernity
BARRY SMART

Racism
ROBERT MILES

Risk
DEBORAH LUPTON

Sexuality
JEFFREY WEEKS

The Symbolic Construction of Community
ANTHONY P. COHEN

ANTI-RACISM

Alastair Bonnett

LONDON AND NEW YORK

First published 2000
by Routledge
11 New Fetter Lane, London EC4P 4EE

Simultaneously published in the USA and Canada
by Routledge
29 West 35th Street, New York, NY 10001

Routledge is an imprint of the Taylor & Francis Group

© 2000 Alastair Bonnett

Typeset in Garamond by Taylor & Francis Books Ltd
Printed and bound in Great Britain by Biddles Ltd, Guildford and King's Lynn

British Library Cataloguing in Publication Data
A catalogue record for this book is available from the British Library

Library of Congress Cataloging in Publication Data
Bonnett, Alastair, 1964–
Anti-racism / Alastair Bonnett
(Key Ideas)
Includes bibliographical references and index.
1. Racism. 2. Race relations. 3. Race awareness.
4. Pluralism (social sciences). 5. Equality. 6. Multicultural education.
I. Title. II. Series.
HT1523.B64   1999   99-32882
305.8–dc21   CIP

ISBN 0–415–17119–9 (hbk)
ISBN 0–415–17120–2 (pbk)

CONTENTS

ACKNOWLEDGEMENTS

Thanks to Mari Shullaw at Routledge for her patience and support for this project.

INTRODUCTION

Anti-racism appears to have a double life. If one were foolish enough to believe everything that was said on the topic, one would be forced to conclude that it is both extraordinarily rare and all-pervasive, simultaneously integral to capitalist modernisation and a harbinger of Marxist revolution. Adding to the sense of confusion that surrounds the subject, debate on anti-racism is often confined to the level of polemic. I have heard anti-racism being celebrated as 'essential' and 'necessary', as well as being attacked as 'politically correct nonsense', even as 'evil'. Adding bewilderment to confusion, the latter epithets all arose from people who prefaced their remarks by claiming to oppose, even to 'hate', racism.

Although such polemical perspectives may have strategic, political justifications, their domination of the subject has made it difficult to approach anti-racism with the historical and socio-logical seriousness it deserves. This is particularly apparent when we contrast the treatment researchers have accorded racism and anti-racism. The myriad ways people racially exclude and oppress each other have been plotted, often with considerable care, many times. The development of societies riven by race and ethnicity is an issue that has attracted attention, attention that has contributed to social change. Whatever reasons may be offered for the consideration paid to the nature of oppression and exclusion and the minimal effort made in understanding the forces of equality, it is clear that an imbalance has been created. Racism and ethnic discriminations are under continuous historical and sociological examination. But anti-racism is consigned to the status of a 'cause', fit only for platitudes of support or denouncement.

This book aims to introduce anti-racism as a topic of social scientific, historical and geographical enquiry. It will show that anti-racism is a global phenomenon, and a diverse social process. Some of the material I will be introducing will be familiar to North American and British readers, but much will not. Indeed, I have consciously steered away from the familiar landmarks of English language anti-racism. The quantity of published work on Martin Luther King, Malcolm X, Nelson Mandela, and the movements associated with them, stands in stark contrast to the dearth of material on struggles elsewhere in the world. It seems that, although many contemporary forms of anti-racism have a theoretical interest in affirming 'diversity', it is a concern rarely translated into an appreciation of the multitude of ways people in different parts of the world resist racism. Thus, the fact that anti-racism exists in Brazil, that its development can be traced in Malaysia, may come as a surprise to those familiar only with the rather insular concerns of debate in the USA or Britain. Yet any text on anti-racism that leaves readers with the impression, either that it is localised to a well-known and limited repertoire of social activism, or that it is an entirely Western activity, another manifestation of Western creativity and egalitarianism, would be both misleading and inadequate.

In recent years the diversity of anti-racism has begun to be recognised. The other two arguments raised in the book may, however, strike readers as more provocative. I shall be suggesting, first, that anti-racism cannot be adequately understood as the inverse of racism. It will be shown that anti-racists have frequently deployed racism to secure and develop their project. The most characteristic form of this incorporation is anti-racists' adherence to categories of 'race'; categories which, even when politically or 'strategically' employed, lend themselves to the racialisation process. The second argument I will be developing takes up the issue of the political complexion of anti-racism. As I have already implied, anti-racism is sometimes seen as a radical form of politics and sometimes as a strategy of control, part and parcel of the effective management of 'cultural diversity'. The political discourses associated with these two tendencies are self-consciously mutually hostile: the former is replete with the language of resistance and struggle while the latter is weighed down with references to social efficiency (for example, the need to maximise the use of human resources), consensus and, increasingly, the barriers racism creates to flexibility in the market place. These two camps are engaged in an undeclared conflict over control of anti-racism. However, it is equally important to note how much they overlap. This is not merely to allude to the frequent co-option of anti-racist radicals by capitalist states. Rather, it is to suggest that the modern state and radical anti-racist movements are contradictory entities that are quite capable of *simultaneously* opening up spaces for both radical and conservative, racialising and anti-essentialist, anti-racist politics.

Although this book takes an inclusive view of its subject, I shall be offering some suggestions as to what form of anti-racism appears most capable of challenging racist knowledges and practices. Thus my analysis of the production of anti-racism as a social and historical process is combined towards the end of the book with a number of admittedly limited but, nevertheless, prescriptive suggestions on the aims and ambitions of anti-racism. More specifically, the case is made for anti-racism as an anti-essentialist political force that acts to denaturalise both ethnic and racial allegiances and categories. I say *both* ethnic and racial very deliberately. The anti-racist challenge to the stereotyping, homogenisation and naturalisation of identity is just as vital among groups commonly called 'ethnic' as it is among those communities who are understood through the terminology of race.

A minimal definition of anti-racism is that it refers to those forms of thought and/or practice that seek to confront, eradicate and/or ameliorate racism. Anti-racism implies the ability to identify a phenomenon – racism – and to do something about it. Of course, different forms of anti-racism often operate with different definitions of what racism is. For example, some construe racism as an articulate, explicit faith in racial superiority, while others view racism as a system of racial discrimination, seeing its key site of operation not within individual consciousness, but in social processes that lead to racial inequality. However, since anti-racism is a negative category, defined in opposition to something considered bad, a good starting point in any attempt to demarcate its different forms is by reference to what it is about racism that anti-racists object to. In other words, what do anti-racists think is wrong with racism? Since racism is almost universally reviled (at least within public discourse) this may seem like a shocking question. Yet, despite the fact that racism appears so unpopular a cause, evidence for its existence remains abundant. In this context the question of how and why people *claim* to be against racism becomes important. There are, after all, few words more likely to evoke angry protestations of innocence than the charge of racism. Moreover, in almost every country, those who explicitly assert racism as an ideology form a relatively tiny and, usually, despised band. Most people, it seems, have some sort of stake in anti-racism. Yet the content and implications of their loyalty vary widely. An identification of commonly expressed reasons why racism is opposed may also provide a useful starting point in thinking about the different social constituencies and functions of anti-racism. Thus, although the list of seven reasons why racism is claimed to be a bad thing offered below is far from exhaustive, it offers a first step in exploring the genesis and forms of anti-racist activism and consciousness.

1   *Racism is socially disruptive.* If racism is regarded as a destabilising influence upon 'good community relations', 'social

cohesion' and 'national unity' it follows that those institutions concerned to maintain or establish these supposed norms will identify it as subversive. Although this form of antipathy to racism is not confined to state agencies and the ruling class, the history of bureaucratic and state anti-racist intervention suggests that, of all the things that are considered bad about racism, it is its power to cause conflict and to 'waste' human resources that most excites the interest of this group. The model of an 'integrated', 'peaceful' and 'tolerant' society tends to be offered as an alternative ideal towards which to strive.

2   *Racism is foreign.* The notion that racism is an alien import, that it has been brought in from outside and represents a malignant foreign body within the national community, is common to many different anti-racist movements. This form of challenge to racism tends to rely on the evocation of 'our' national history as marked by equality, tolerance and/or pluralism and the claim that another society is the natural home, as well as the prime source, of racist ideas. Within Europe in the mid and late twentieth century the latter role was frequently assigned to Germany. However, this kind of 'othering' of racism has also informed certain anti-colonial and anti-Western discourses. It is particularly apparent in the suggestion that any signs or symptoms of racism identified outside the West represent an entirely alien contamination, a manifestation of colonialism that can be opposed by 'indigenous traditions'.

3   *Racism sustains the ruling class.* This concern serves to remind us that opposition to racism can arise from a hostility to other social practices and ideologies considered to be of a more fundamental nature. The notion, commonly found within class struggle politics (Marxist and anarchist), that racism is an important element in the glue that holds the ruling class in power relies on a representation of racism as dividing the working class and inculcating within them conservative ideologies.

4   *Racism hinders the progress of 'our community'.* Most opposition to

racism has arisen from its victims. These kinds of struggle draw on each of the concerns with racism identified above and below. However, they also often mobilise another claim, that of self-interest. In such cases the problem with racism is seen as its power to prevent 'our community' (who may or may not be self-identified in racial terms) from developing economically and socially. Racism is cast as a barrier, the dismantling of which will enable 'full participation' in society, most especially participation within mainstream and elite economic and occupational roles from which the victim group has been barred or marginalised.

5   *Racism is an intellectual error.* The science of race has long been accused of being an example of the misuse of scientific method. However, it was the mid to late twentieth century that saw the credibility and authority of scientific racism collapse. This has enabled the notion that racism is 'bad science' and is based on mistakes of fact and judgement to secure its place within many forms of anti-racist discourse. It also allows the advocates of racism to be cast as the ignorant articulators of an anachronistic ideology. However, the ignorance of such individuals is also often understood as being rooted in their lack of familiarity and knowledge of 'others'. This latter critique suggests that the mistake of racism is its blinkered ethnocentrism, a world-view that is contrasted with the more cosmopolitan perspective of the anti-racist.

6   *Racism distorts and erases people's identities.* This concern, which may be identified in nearly all forms of anti-racism, is usually considered to take place within the individual psyche as well as at a collective level. Although not necessarily directed towards those who are the victims of racism, this form of analysis is commonly focused upon the destructive power racism has upon people's notions of and ability to politically deploy 'their own' history, culture and sense of social cohesion. If the victim group is seen as a race, then racism will be cast as subverting that community's ability to express and fulfil their racial identity. Alternatively, the identification of races and racial attributes may be cast *as part of* the

destructive logic of racism. In this view, it is the ability of racists to fabricate and disseminate racial logic and categories that should generate opposition.

7   *Racism is anti-egalitarian and socially unjust.* Egalitarianism and notions of social justice are deployed at some level within most forms of anti-racism. However, to extend this observation into the claim that these are the dominant reasons people oppose racism would be unwise. Nevertheless, this form of opposition to racism usually draws on what are often cast as 'deeply held' political and/or religious convictions that all people are, at some fundamental level, equal. An associated assertion that people have inalienable rights, one of which is the right not to be the victim of racism, is often allied to this form of egalitarianism.

Although each of these seven concerns is usually found in combination, the last three mentioned may, arguably, be deemed to be inherent within the anti-racist project. This claim relies on the fact that all three appear, in some form or another, in nearly all forms of anti-racism and that it is difficult to 'think anti-racism', to participate in anti-racist discourse, without using them. More specifically, they are commonly deployed as the moral core and intellectual baseline of anti-racism. In the sense that they represent shared ideals, a commonly held aspiration concerning what anti-racism should be about, we might wish to say that the closer anti-racism comes to embodying these three ambitions the more authentic, the more anti-racist, it can be deemed. However, it must also be noted that claims to 'the intellectual truth of anti-racism', 'the right of people "to be who they are"' and 'human equality' do not represent a necessarily cohesive set of opinions. One site of potential tension is the status of race in each of these discourses. For if we accept that the notion of race is an intellectual error and a cause of both inequality and the destruction of identity, then it follows that enabling people to express their own racial identity and to be accorded equality, and rights, *as races* is problematic. Another point of tension arises between the relativism of enabling everyone to 'be themselves', a process that necessarily entails 'respecting' social, cultural and, potentially racial, dissimilarities, and the universalism of the claim of human equality. In the latter instance it is the sameness of people that matters, in the former their differences. The tension between relativist and universalist interpretations of the struggle against racism provides one of the continuous threads within anti-racist debate. Indeed, it is a tension that pre-dates the invention of the term 'anti-racism'. As Chapter 1 shows, the ideological antecedents of anti-racism were already marked by many of the ambivalences and disputes that surround the topic today.

1

ROOTS OF RESISTANCE

The antecedents and ambivalences of anti-racism

INTRODUCTION

Where does anti-racism come from? This question is not of merely historical interest. Constructions of the past play an important role in all forms of anti-racism, both as a site of legitimation and by providing examples of what racism is and where it leads. History is constantly deployed by anti-racists. But it is equally true that many of the tensions within contemporary anti-racism were also apparent within the traditions it seeks to claim. More specifically, the tensions between relativist and universalist visions of equality can be seen to weave their way through the history of both the Enlightenment, Western identified, 'anti-racist heritage' and non-Western and/or anti-Western identified traditions of anti-colonialism and anti-imperialism. As this implies, this chapter shows that racism and anti-racism are often intermingled, even inseparable, tendencies. Such a portrait of moral complexity contrasts with more sentimental accounts, in which the story of anti-racism is staged as a melodrama, the characters presented as heroes and villains: pure anti-racists versus pure racists, good against evil. Such an approach has its place. But this book is not one of them. This is not an account of super-humans, of anti-racist martyrs and saints, of people capable of extracting themselves from the norms of their day. The narrative developed here is far more politically messy; peopled, as it is, by individuals struggling *within and against* their social context.

The first problem that any history of anti-racism must confront is a basic one. The term 'anti-racism' is a twentieth-century creation. Indeed, it did not appear in regular usage until the 1960s (and even then it was largely confined to English- and French-speaking countries). Its development during this decade accompanied a number of other new forms of emancipatory discourse, such as anti-sexism and gay rights. The apparent novelty of anti-racism partly explains why it has rarely been situated within a broader historical and sociological context. However, although the term is new, much of its symbolic power relies on its ability to draw on ideas, such as human equality and cultural relativism, of considerable age. The linguistic history of the term should, perhaps, also be extended back, as far as the 1930s, the period when *The Oxford English Dictionary* (1989) cites the first usage of both 'racism' (1932) and 'racist' (1936) (the use of 'racialism' is found earlier, in 1902). All these categories were first employed as terms of criticism. As this suggests, the concept of racism was conceived by those who opposed it, by *anti*-racists. Strictly speaking, any attempt to portray *anti*-racism before this time, *before* the concept of racism existed, is anachronistic.

It is precisely this sense of anachronism that makes a book like Herbert Aptheker's (1993) *Anti-racism in U.S. History: The First Two Hundred Years* appear to be suffering from what historians call 'presentism'. In other words, it tries to explain the past through the ideas and categories of the present. A chronology of centuries of anti-racist activity, a chronology in which a discrete and stable thing, 'racism', is attacked in various ways, by various people, year after year, will, inevitably, be misleading. Historical enquiries in this area are necessarily limited to locating influences and tendencies that have fed into the formation of twentieth- and twenty-first century anti-racism and/or may be judged, as far as possible, in their own terms, to have resisted ideologies of racial domination.

A note about my use of the word 'Western' may be useful before proceeding. My practice in this book is not to frame terms in scare quotes simply because they are problematic (if I followed that course, these pages would soon darken with swarms of inverted commas). However, wherever possible, I have sought to provoke suspicion about claims for the existence of homogeneous and distinct Western and non-Western spheres of ideological creation. Whichever way they are written, the use of these labels has the unfortunate consequence of both guiding attention away from the mutually constitutive nature of emancipatory activity in different parts of the world, and of setting up the 'non-West' as merely the negation, the 'non', of the 'West'. It is indicative of the complexity of the debate, of the difficulty of finding any unproblematic position from which to speak, that although my account will attempt to expose and undermine these categories, they remain necessary, if only because they continue to animate and structure so much contemporary anti-racism.

RELATIVISM, UNIVERSALISM AND THE IDEA OF PREJUDICE IN WESTERN THOUGHT

The relationship of anti-racism to traditions of egalitarianism and tolerance within Western thought is a controversial, politically charged, issue. On the one hand, we find these traditions regularly employed to legitimise the notion that there exists a benign, emancipatory, dynamic within Western modernity. Within Western societies this assertion (which is sometimes accompanied by the stronger claim that the first anti-racists were thinkers from the European Enlightenment) has been evoked to popularise anti-racism and to encourage European heritage peoples to feel that it is not a foreign or threatening idea. Yet, on the other hand, there is something immediately suspect about claiming anti-racism 'for the West'. In an unsettling mutation of European colonialism, the notions of liberation, emancipation, and resistance become gifts of 'civilisation', to be thankfully received by more 'primitive' cultures; peoples, races, who have failed to produce their own Montaigne or Marx. As we shall see, the strain between these interpretations is unlikely to be resolved, for both egalitarianism and discrimination, anti-racism and racism, are woven together within the West's visions of equality and tolerance.

The most subtle identification of this double history may be found within the work of the French sociologist Pierre-André Taguieff. In *Les Fins de l'antiracisme* (1995) and *La Force du préjugé* (1988) Taguieff traces the contradictions of anti-racism within French thought, constantly emphasising the way it has been simultaneously an exclusive and inclusive tradition, both racist and anti-racist. However, despite possessing a depth unequalled in the English-language literature, Taguieff's studies rarely raise their sights above France and, occasionally, the USA. Anti-racism is portrayed by Taguieff as a problematic of the West, a product of Western thinkers, Western actions. The inadequacy of any attempt to trace a discrete Western tradition of anti-racism finds historical support within recent studies that have shown that many of the Western intellectuals Taguieff associates with the critique of racial prejudice sought sanction for their ideas in Eastern thought. Thus, for example, in *Oriental Enlightenment* Clarke (1997) traces how, from the eighteenth century, European studies of consciousness and spirituality, as well as technical inventions and bureaucratic procedures, were legitimised by reference to Chinese and Indian influence and sagacity. The nature of this influence is beyond the scope of the present book, but is a useful reminder that the categories Western and non-Western denote processes of identity formation rather than objective and discrete social realms.

Within the geographical area that, from the eighteenth century, became known as 'Europe' two discourses emerged that have often been aligned to the assertion of equality, namely, relativism and universalism. The debate between these positions is far from over. Indeed, many studies of contemporary anti-racism structure their subject matter into universalist and relativist approaches. These, Taguieff (1995, p. 357) writes, are the 'two great orientations of anti-racism'. Indeed, Wieviorka (1997, p. 147) refers to 'the opposition between the contradictory universalist and the differentialist [i.e. relativist] orientations of anti-racist action' as 'structural problems which constantly undermine anti-racist action'. I shall introduce each of these tendencies in turn, elaborating on the connections between, and contradictions within, them.

Relativism

Relativism refers to the belief that truths are situationally dependent. In the context of debate on racial equality it refers, more specifically, to the idea that cultural and/or physical differences between races should be recognised and respected; that different does not mean unequal. Relativism has a long history. Its assertion has often been associated with the attempt to interpret 'other peoples' by an imperial power. Relativism usually performs this function, and is defined in relation to, the chauvinistic or supremacist traditions also generated within colonial societies. As this implies, relativism is rarely the only, or indeed the dominant, mode of cross-cultural interpretation at work within the context of expansionism. Thus, for example, it was both *within and against* the norms of Roman imperial discourse for the philosopher Lucius Seneca (4BC–AD65) to instruct that

> Among his own people the colour of the Ethiopian is not notable, and amongst the Germans red hair gathered into a knot is not unseemly for a man. You are to count nothing odd or disgraceful for an individual which is a general characteristic of his nation.
>
> (quoted by Snowden, 1983, pp. 86–87)

The modern tradition of relativism is often traced back to the European Renaissance, more specifically to the writings of Michel de Montaigne (1533–1592). Montaigne used the European encounter with the New World to challenge the notion that

French manners and customs were superior. Reviewing a variety of social practices from around the world, he noted, in his essay 'On habit', that the 'laws of conscience which we say are born of Nature, are born of custom' (1993, p. 130). In the same composition Montaigne wrote that

> A man who wished to loose himself from the violent foregone conclusions of custom will find many things accepted as being indubitably settled which have nothing to support them but the hoary whiskers and wrinkles of attendant usage; let him tear off that mask, bring matters back to truth and reason, and he will feel his judgement turned upside-down, yet restored by this to a much surer state.
>
> (ibid., p. 132)

Montaigne may be said to have sought to expose the workings of what today we call racial or cultural 'bias'. His own position – as someone who claimed the capability of rising above such limitations – is that of the cosmopolitan, an individual of broader horizons than the blinkered masses and conservative elite. Montaigne's best-known engagement with social prejudice came in his essay concerning Brazilian coastal peoples, 'On the cannibals'. His account was entirely drawn from secondary sources. Montaigne was not so much interested in providing a factual depiction of another culture, or the reality of cannibalism, as in asserting that even the most seemingly bizarre and exotic of social practices can be explained, rationalised and justified, if understood within their social context.

> I find (from what has been told to me) that there is nothing savage or barbarous about those peoples, but that every man calls barbarous anything he is not accustomed to; it is indeed the case that we have no other criterion of truth or right-reason than the example and form of the opinions and customs of our own country. There we always find the perfect religion, the perfect polity, the most developed and perfect way of doing anything!
>
> (ibid., p. 231)

In the same essay Montaigne goes on to offer a contrast between the uncorrupted condition of New World peoples and the decadence of French society. It is at this juncture that we encounter an intriguing characteristic of the relativist tradition. For at its most socially critical moments it often draws on, or asserts, the existence of supposedly *universal* principles of conduct and action. Thus, for example, when most celebratory of his 'cannibals', and most critical of French society, Montaigne relies on a construct of Nature, of the natural, as a universal 'good thing'. The French, he claims, are no longer at one with Nature, they are alienated from Nature, but

> 'savages' are only wild in the sense that we call fruits wild when they are produced by Nature in the ordinary course: whereas it is fruit which we have artificially perverted and misled from the common order which we ought to call savage.
> (ibid., p. 231)

Montaigne was aware that his affirmations of otherness were essentially reactions to French society and had very little to do with the realities of other peoples: 'I do not speak the minds of others', he wrote, 'except to speak my own mind better' (cited by Todorov, 1993, p. 41). In this respect Montaigne's work exemplifies a wider trend: the growth and popularity of cultural relativism among intellectual circles in Europe from the late seventeenth century were dependent upon its utility as a method of critiquing European society.

One of the most influential ways European relativists articulated their position was by writing fictional narratives of non-European travellers' perceptions of Europe. These accounts were used as forms of political satire on the conservatism and arrogance of European institutions. The most famous example of this type of literature is Montesquieu's *Persian Letters* (1973, first published 1721). Montesquieu's work consists of a series of letters, seemingly composed by two Persian travellers, called Usbek and Rica. The letters discuss national differences within Europe, constantly expressing surprise and interest in the *exotic* and *peculiar* nature of European customs. The contemporary critic Tzvetan Todorov asserts that Montesquieu 'incorporates the most successful effort within the French tradition to conceptualise the diversity of peoples and the unity of the human race at one and the same time' (1993, p. 353). It is certainly true that Montesquieu sought to expose prejudice which he defined, in *The Spirit of the Laws*, as 'what makes one unaware of oneself' (1989, p. xliv) and assert the importance of cultural defamiliarisation. The attempt to demonstrate the particularity and, indeed, the oddness, of French and European culture, which lies at the heart of the *Persian Letters*, is a classic statement of this latter technique. It is a project that adopts the figure of the stranger, the foreigner, as a uniquely valuable and attentive individual, someone who is not blinded by prejudice. 'You who, being a foreigner', a 'candid' French acquaintance suggests to Rica, 'want to know about things, and know them as they are' (ibid., p. 239).

From defamiliarisation sprout the fruits of relativism, namely tolerance and self-knowledge. The first is exemplified by Usbek's remarks on religion: 'since in every religion there are precepts which are useful to society, it is well they should be obeyed with enthusiasm, and what is more likely to encourage this enthusiasm than a multiplicity of religions?' (ibid., p. 165).

Self-knowledge, the other product of defamiliarisation, necessarily entails understanding the socially located limits of one's own knowledge and the refusal of suprematicism. Rica writes to his friend:

> It seems to me, Usbek, that all our judgements are made with reference covertly to ourselves. I do not find it surprising that the negroes paint the devil sparkling white, and their gods black as coal ... It has been well said that if triangles had a god, they would give him three sides.
>
> (ibid., p. 124)

The dislocative power of Montesquieu's account encouraged similar attempts to write from the perspective of outsiders in European society. Other examples include Goldsmith's *Citizen of the World: or Letters from a Chinese Philosopher Residing in London to His Friend in the East* (1934, first published 1762) and Marat's *Polish Letters* (1971; written in the 1770s, first published 1905) which follows the fortunes of a Polish traveller to the 'civilised countries' of Western Europe (see Wolff, 1994, for discussion). The primitivist conceit of the latter text is equally apparent in Voltaire's *L'Ingénu* (1964, first published 1756) which critiqued French society from the point of view of a Breton boy brought up by the Huron Indians. On returning to France, 'The Child of Nature', as Voltaire calls him, manages to overturn and expose the intolerance of French elite society. Even a wise hermit he encounters in prison has to admit, 'I shall never obtain the natural commonsense of this half-savage boy! I fear I have been hard at work strengthening prejudices, whereas he listens only to nature' (ibid., p. 150).

However, although such works appear benign affirmations of cultural tolerance, relativism does not have an unambiguous relationship to the quest for human equality. It is instructive to observe that in *The Spirit of the Laws* (1989; first published 1748) Montesquieu comfortably combined his relativism with a series of highly negative stereotypes of Indians, Africans and other non-European peoples. As this implies, respecting difference can easily turn into asserting hierarchy. The conservative potential within relativism was noted by Rousseau, who drew particular attention to the inability of such work to move beyond the political agendas of Europe. In his *Discourse on Inequality* (1984, first published 1755), Rousseau writes:

> In the two or three centuries since the inhabitants of Europe have been flooding into other parts of the world, endlessly publishing new collections of voyages and travel, I am persuaded that we have come to know no other men except Europeans; moreover it appears from the ridiculous prejudices, which have not died out even among men of letters, that every author produces under the pompous name of the study of man nothing much more than the study of men of his own country.

(1984, p. 159)

Rousseau casts doubt not on the idea of relativism itself, but on Europeans' employment of it to sustain their own sense of cultural superiority. It is a critique that suggests that relativism has often been accompanied by the decidedly unrelativist assumption that European values and habits are the yardstick that the world can and must be measured against; that Europe is the fixed norm that defines other cultures as exotic. The contemporary critic, Homi Bhabha, locates this condescending attitude as characteristic of European claims to cultural sophistication and cosmopolitanism:

> In fact the sign of the 'cultured' or the 'civilised' attitude is the ability to appreciate cultures in a kind of *musée imaginaire*; as though one should be able to collect and appreciate them. Western connoisseurship is the capacity to understand and locate cultures in a universal time-frame that acknowledges their various historical and social contexts only eventually to transcend them and render them transparent.

(1990, p. 208)

Thus, the relativist project is accused of bad faith; of being unwilling to place Europe itself within the relativist maelstrom to which all other cultures are consigned. Other critics of relativism have drawn attention to the social implications of its emphasis and affirmation of human difference (Todorov, 1993; Malik, 1996). Such ideas, they point out, far from enabling racial equality, encourage racial exclusion and denigration. Indeed, the twentieth century is filled with examples, from Nazism to apartheid, of the use of the notion of 'respecting difference' to justify destruction of cultures and peoples. Asserting relativism's complicity with racism Todorov notes simply that the 'absence of unity allows exclusion, which can lead to extermination' (1993, p. 389).

This anti-relativist stance is, in part, generated by the association of studies of human difference with racial science. It draws, then, on the reality that for many nineteenth-century racial scientists the fact that difference had to be respected was the same thing as saying that racial *in*equality had to be respected. However, the connection between racial science and racism should not be used to obscure the complexities of the relativist position. A clear example of such ambiguity is presented in the work of one of the forefathers of racial science, the man who invented the term 'Caucasian', Johann Blumenbach (1752–1840). Blumenbach was a pioneer of the categorisation of people into races. He was also an ardent opponent of slavery, and gathered voluminous material to prove the skill and intelligence of Africans in the arts, literature and science. Thus, Aptheker (1993), noting only his interest in African culture, claims Blumenbach as an anti-racist. However, Eze (1997), citing his work in racial science, categorises him as a racist. What neither interpretation permits is an understanding of the intertwining, mutually constitutive, nature of what we today term 'racism' and 'anti-racism', either in Blumenbach's work or, more broadly, within the relativist tradition in Western thought.

Universalism

Universalism may be defined, in contrast to relativism, as the assertion of the validity, across all cultures or historical periods, of certain values, truths and processes. Within anti-racist discourses it is often associated with the conviction that people are all equally part of humanity and should all be accorded the same rights and opportunities. As this implies, the notion of prejudice is as central in universalist discourse as it is in relativism. However, the emphasis within universalism is on the task of over-coming prejudice in order to see and enable the equality, the sameness, of people, rather than on conquering prejudice in the name of difference. The 'universalist utopia' of the Enlightenment tradition, Taguieff asserts, is 'the dream of a world without prejudices' (1988, p. 188). Referring to the revo-lutionary socialist Pierre Leroux's declaration of 1841 that 'the prejudice of race is abolished ... all men are equal', Taguieff links universalism to the attempt to expound a modern, secular perspective based on the assertion of a common human nature and a common set of rights:

> it is one of the innumerable pronouncements, more or less triumphalist, that infers from the progressive optimism of the eighteenth century the need for a final end to the reign of prejudice ... The common conceit of [the great modern political doctrines] is their power to lead men beyond servitude, from the shadows of ignorance, from slavery and superstition ... this general movement of emancipation is universalist, for it cannot tolerate any exception ... To fulfil its mission it must be total.
>
> (1988, pp. 192–193)

Science is often understood as the archetypal universalist discourse. It is logical to assume that if science is objective, if it is for eternal truths and against bias, it must be against prejudice, including racial prejudice. And, despite the fact that racial science was one of the origins of the doctrine of biological racism, both the nineteenth and twentieth centuries saw the authority and testament of science being drawn on to oppose racism. It is interesting to note in this regard that the increasing association, from the end of the nineteenth century, and most especially after the Second World War, of racial thinking with unreason led many who wished to align themselves with the authentic spirit of science to position 'real science' as *inherently* anti-racist. Indeed, the representation of racism as a perversion of 'real science' was established as a scientific orthodoxy from the mid-twentieth century (Barkan, 1992).

And yet, the attempt to align science with anti-racism obscures the fact that the former's core ideology, universalism, has had an ambiguous relationship with racial discrimination. More specifically, the universalist tradition may be seen as, at one and the same time, an emancipatory force and part and parcel of the colonial and neo-colonial imposition of Western values and norms. This argument may be usefully contrasted with recent attempts to root anti-racism firmly within 'the universalist tradition'. Malik, for example, writes: 'The enlightenment belief in a common, universal human nature tended to undermine any proclivity for a racial categorisation of humanity' (1996, p. 53). Malik supports his thesis by reference to examples of relativist positions of a clearly reactionary nature. Thus, for example, he cites the French conservative Joseph de Maistre (1753–1821) mocking the revolutionary attachment to 'the rights of Man':

> There is no such thing as *man* in the world. During my life I have seen Frenchmen, Italians, Russians, and so on; thanks to Montesquieu I even know that one can be *Persian*; but I must say, as for *man*, I have never come across him anywhere; if he exists he is completely unknown to me.
>
> (ibid., p. 266)

Malik's use of de Maistre's pronouncement is designed to suggest the essentially progressive nature of the Enlightenment construct of universal 'Man'. The very notion of equality, Malik implies, demands the assertion of an equivalence between people, a commonality of experience, worth and values. Malik reminds us that these ideas have inspired revolutionaries and egalitarians around the world. Yet the relationship of universalism to non-European emancipation is less straightforward than he admits. We can explore the complex political energies within universalism through the work of two highly influential nineteenth-century universalists, Comte and Marx. Both men have been drawn into contemporary accounts of the development of anti-racism (for example, Taguieff, 1988, 1995) and both exemplify the Enlightenment conviction in the possibility of universally valid acts of reason and judgement. Both men asserted the fundamental equality of the races of the world, drawing all of humanity into their schemes for global transformation. Each also considered that 'backward' and pre-modern societies were doomed to a necessary extinction.

In his *Système de politique positive* (1851–1854) the French socialist and positivist, Auguste Comte, set out a vision of a world governed by universal laws. 'The fundamental laws of human evolution', he wrote, 'which establish the philosophical basis of the ultimate regime, are necessarily appropriate to all climates and all races, except for mere differences in speed' (1851, p. 390). Comte offered a bold utopian model for the rational and egalitarian transformation of all societies. He envisioned a secular, unified, globe governed by 'liberty' (which he called 'the religion of Humanity') and reason. Indeed, Comte's belief that logic, particularly mathematical logic, provided the bedrock upon which a just society could be founded led him to aver that all phenomena are 'logically able to be represented by an equation' (cited by Taguieff, 1988, p. 211).

Comte's fantasy of equality involved the expansion of a regime rooted in the principles and policies of the French Enlightenment ('the core of humanity') across Europe and, then, across the planet (for discussion, see Todorov, 1993). First, other European heritage people would feel the benefits of incorporation into French liberty, then Asians and, finally, Africans. For Comte racial harmony and equality and white, not to say French, supremacy advanced hand in hand: 'The total harmony of the Great-Being thus requires the intimate cooperation of its three races', he noted, adding, 'The human presidency is irrevocably conferred on the West' (1854, p. 365).

Comte appears to contemporary eyes as an anti-racist racist. Can the same be said of Karl Marx? The works of Marx have often been drawn on within anti-racist debate. The emancipatory logic found within his analysis of capitalism, with its promise of universal liberation in communism, has influenced the way notions of equality and radical social change have been understood across the world. Indeed, although he wrote hardly anything on race, Marx has sometimes been drawn into the pantheon of anti-colonial thinkers. This depiction may, in part, be justified by reference to his contention that 'the secret of the impotence of the English working class' was the 'antagonism ... artificially sustained and intensified by the press, the pulpit, the comic papers' between English and Irish workers in Britain (Marx, 1974, p. 169). It is also pertinent to mention the numerous articles Marx wrote for the *New York Daily Tribune* and other newspapers in the 1850s on the injustices of British inter-vention in India and China. He roundly condemned the 'Christianity-canting and civilization-mongering British Government' (Marx, 1969, p. 347) both for its barbarity and for its hypocrisy. 'Another civilization war' (Marx, 1859) was the bitterly ironic title of one of his later dispatches on the British government's plans for military incursion in China. However, like Comte, Marx's egalitarianism was also premised on the conviction that there existed a linear, evolutionary, pathway to social trans-formation and that Western society provided a model for the whole of humanity. Indeed, despite his hostility to British barbarism, Marx regarded colonial conquest by the West as desir-able. Only the destruction of 'traditional' societies and their replacement with new, modern, social processes and forces, Marx argued, would enable people to achieve class consciousness and the material conditions required for communist revolution. He explained: 'England has to fulfil a double mission in India: one destructive, the other regenerating – the annihilation of old Asiatic society, and the laying of the material foundations of Western society in Asia' (1992, p. 320).

The 'idyllic village communities' characteristic of the East, Marx claimed, 'restrain the human mind within the smallest possible compass ... enslaving it beneath traditional rules, depriving it of all grandeur and historical energies' (ibid., p. 306). In order for history to dawn within Asia, and other non-Western societies, they must be subject to the revolution that, for Marx, is inaugurated by Western colonialism.

> England, it is true, in causing a social revolution in Hindustan was actuated only by the vilest interests, and was stupid in her manner of enforcing them. But that is not the question. The question is, can mankind fulfil its destiny without a funda-mental revolution in the social state of Asia? If not, whatever may have been the crimes of England she was the uncon-scious tool of history in bringing about that revolution.
>
> (ibid., p. 307)

Ultimately, for Marx, as for Comte, the question that must be asked of European domination was not 'does it oppress?' or 'is it unjust?', but 'is it the agent of History?'. Comte's and Marx's universalism relied on according Europe the position of civilising centre, of the cockpit of history, the place where human liberation and equality are defined and from where they are disseminated. The universalist promise of equality demands the submission, the self-obliteration, of those to whom it is 'offered'. 'We can all be one', 'we can all be equal', it is suggested, 'if you become like me'. 'The most fundamental prejudice', Taguieff wryly observes, 'resides in the belief of not having any prejudices' (1995, p. 197).

RESISTING, ADAPTING AND ENGAGING WESTERN RACISM

Neither racism nor colonialism are inherently Western things. Indeed, both have characterised expansionist campaigns and nationalist ideologies in many societies in the modern era, from East Asia to South America. However, the fact that the race concept was invented in the West and the extraordinary power of Western racism and colonialism fully explain why these ideas are so often associated with the West. It also justifies, I would suggest, this section's focus on resistance to and engagement with these Western forms.

The expansion of European peoples and European influence across the globe has been resisted in myriad ways by those whom Europeans designated as racial inferiors. Anti-colonialism and anti-racism are intimately related political projects precisely because the principal impact of racism on the world has been within colonial and neo-colonial contexts. Colonialism was legitimised through racism, and vice versa. Indeed, in the modern period, anti-colonial struggles have nearly always also been struggles against racial/ethnic domination. This resistance has, moreover, often been articulated as an alliance, a shared struggle, of subject races. As expressed in the campaigning newspaper, the *Jamaica Advocate*, in 1904, 'famine and oppression' may be the lot of colonised races, but

The subject races were not always governed by that spirit ...
the Indian will some day repel the assumption, the African will
do the same thing, the Egyptian and Burmese etc., will vindi-
cate their individuality and will prove that temporary
dominance is not evidence of constitutional superiority.

(cited by Lewis, 1987, p. 35)

Opposition to racism may be found from China to South
America, from the Middle East to the Arctic: the roots of resistance are global and polyvocal. In an attempt to exemplify this
diversity, while providing examples of some of the most important forms of opposition, I will introduce four anti-racist
antecedents from different parts of the world. In order to provide
a focus for these studies each will be organised around the work of
one particular individual or group of activists. The four studies
have, in part, been chosen because they each reflect concerns of
contemporary anti-racism. My focus on particular individuals and
groups should not be read as an attempt to propound a 'great
men' view of anti-racist and anti-colonial history (cf. the self-
explanatory title of Tinker's *Men Who Overturned Empires: Fighters,
Dreamers and Schemers*, 1987). The men that form the focus of my
account (and on maleness of anti-racist historiography see Carby,
1998; also Chapter 4) have been chosen because they illustrate a
particular perspective on the meaning and implications of being
oppressed by racism. However 'great' they may or may not have
been, it is not their fame but their ideas that concern us here.

Despite their diversity, each of these portraits suggests that the
notion of 'resistance' is not a completely adequate way of understanding the way Western racism has been engaged. Indeed, as
we shall see, some of the different traditions isolated below
adopted something very much like racism as part of their 'anti-
racism', while others drew on conservative or European
Enlightenment traditions to struggle against Western dominance. Like the Western traditions discussed earlier, non-Western
'proto-anti-racism' is characterised by ambivalence and contradiction.

José Vasconcelos, hybridity and the cosmic race

If we accept that one of the core characteristics of racism is a belief in racial purity, it would seem sensible to suppose that any assertion of the beneficial effects of miscegenation would represent a challenge to this tradition. Indeed, over recent years, some contemporary Western anti-racists have begun drawing on the Latin American language of race mixture to express their belief that hybridity represents an escape from, and form of subversion of, the racialisation process (cf. Young, 1995; Sakamoto, 1996). Thus they assert that 'foregrounding the *mestizo* factor' inevitably and always 'valorises boundary crossing' (Pieterse, 1995, p. 543) and, hence, characterises the most advanced forms of anti-racist thinking and practice. However, the anti-racist status of traditions of race mixture in Latin America is far more problematic than such appropriations allow.

The history of Spanish and Portuguese colonial incursion into the Americas offers some of the earliest examples of the assertion of, and resistance to, 'racism'. Hierarchical distinctions between racial groups were inscribed by these two European powers in legal and economic conduct within their American dominions from the sixteenth century. At the apex of this configuration stood the white Christian settler. Below him or her other 'primary types' were identified, as well as a bewildering variety of racial mixtures (demarcations in Spanish-speaking Latin America included 'chinos' ('Negro' and 'Indian' parentage), 'zambos' ('mulattos' and 'Negro' parentage) and 'zambo–chino' ('chino' and 'Negro' parentage). The baroque complexity of this system of categorisation appears to have been a factor in undermining its long-term sustainability. This interpretation is supported by the fact that, from the late nineteenth century, the full array of racial categories was increasingly deemed too complex to incorporate into the routines of everyday life and was gradually marginalised as archaic. However, the survival of stereotypes of whiteness, blackness and 'indigenousness' as structuring norms within American societies should warn against conflating this history with the decline of racism. The continuing and diverse struggles against racism in Latin America give the lie to the romantic delusion that Latin American nations are 'racial democracies'.

Three of the most important elements in this history are anti-colonialism and the ideologies of 'indigenism' (*indigenismo*) and *mestizaje* (a Spanish term denoting the ideology and the practice of racial mixture). Each of these factors has an ambiguous relationship to the racialisation process. Anti-colonial, and more especially national liberation, movements in Latin America advanced critiques of Spanish and Portuguese racial suprematicism, critiques that were, in part, encouraged by the ideals of the European Enlightenment. Emphasising the latter relationship, Polanco (1997, p. 11) notes that many of the national liberators were 'steeped in the ideas of Rousseau, Encyclopedism and the great ideals of freedom, equality and democracy advanced by the North American and French revolutions'. Perhaps not unrelatedly, the main agents of national liberation, and the main beneficiaries, were the creole (i.e. European heritage) elite. The cultural and racial ambitions of the creole elites who dominated the independence movements have been summarised by Mary Louise Pratt (1992). The 'liberal Creole project', she explains, 'involved founding an independent, decolonised American society and culture, while retaining European values and white supremacy' (ibid., p. 175). The development of the ideology of *mestizaje* both accompanied and challenged this project. As Martin Lienhard (1997; see also Mallon, 1996) argues, the double movement of *mestizaje* between racism and anti-racism reflects its ideological role within the forging of Latin American national identity. Indeed, Lienhard extends this observation to claim that

> The paradigm of 'mestizaje' is no more, in reality, than an ideological discourse whose purpose is to justify the hegemony of national creole groups who assumed power when the colonial system fell apart. In the midst of a political transition characterised by its mechanism of discrimination and exclusion, the ideologeme of cultural 'mestizaje' served, above all, to postulate the equality – whilst hiding the inequality – of the groups composing the different national societies. In a word,

> 'mestizaje' is the product and the instrument of a racist ideology.
>
> (ibid., p. 189)

In fact, although Lienhard's cynicism may be politically apt, it tends to obscure the contradictory momentum within *mestizaje*. The interwoven nature of racism and anti-racism, relativism and universalism, within *mestizaje* can be traced throughout its history, including within the thought of the Liberator, Simón Bolívar. Writing in 1815 Bolívar asserted the importance of both establishing 'legal equality' between the races and of breaking away from notions of racial purity. 'We are', he explained, 'neither Indian nor European, but a species midway between the legitimate proprietors of this country and the Spanish usurpers.' Yet Bolívar was later to associate a lack of 'purity' with conflict and inferiority. Proposing a 'natural enmity of the colours', he noted that South America is 'very far from the wonderful times of Athens and Rome, and we must not compare ourselves in any way to anything European. The origins of our existence are most impure' (cited by Mörner, 1967, pp. 86–87).

However, the clearest manifestations of the interconnection between the acceptance and rejection of European claims to superiority were to emerge with the institutionalisation of *mestizaje* as a national ideology and identity. In Mexico *mestizaje* became allied to the nation-building ambitions of the post-1910 revolutionary regime. It also became associated with the new government's attempts to assimilate native peoples and native symbols into the national project, a process that was undertaken under the banner of *indigenismo*. In Mexico this combination came together in what Knight (1990, p. 86) calls a 'new indigenista–mestizaje cult' of national integration. 'In the great forge of the Americas', wrote one of the principal advocates of *mestizaje* as an official, national ideology, Manuel Gamio (cited by Knight, 1990, p. 85), 'on the giant anvil of the Andes, virile races of bronze and iron have struggled for centuries', producing a new 'national race', the *mestizo*, the basis of the 'national culture of the future'. However, it is Gamio's colleague José Vasconcelos whose name is most closely associated with this project. Minister for Education between 1921 and 1924, Vasconcelos is best remembered today as the man who commissioned the wall murals that adorn some of Mexico City's public buildings, murals that integrate revolutionary class politics with new national myths organised around native images and legends. Vasconcelos was also the author of a number of studies that sought to tie anti-colonialism with the ideology of 'the cosmic race'. In direct opposition to notions of racial purism and European supremacy, Vasconcelos drew on established traditions of race mixing in Latin America to propose that racial hybridisation was the only way forward for humankind. Thus Vasconcelos identified European racism not simply as an imperialist ideology but one that was subversive of the attempt to develop a new and better form of civilisation in Latin America:

> The British preach natural selection, with the tacit conclusion that world domination belongs, by natural and divine law, to the dolichocephalous man from the Isles and his descendants. But this science, which invaded us with the artifacts of conquering commerce, is fought as all imperialism is fought: by confronting it with a superior science, and with a broader and more vigorous civilisation.
>
> (1997, pp. 33–34)

Vasconcelos's critique of European racial hierarchies was highly influential when first published in *La raza cósmica* ('The Cosmic Race') in 1925 (1997). Moreover, his ideas affirming racial hybridity find echoes in the national myths developed within a variety of modern Latin American societies. However, Vasconcelos's reputation in Mexico has suffered considerably in recent years. To understand why we need to appreciate the ambiguous character of his thinking on race. For, like so much of the material I am introducing in this chapter, Vasconcelos's 'anti-racism' was enabled and structured by his 'racism'. The notion of hybridisation he employed relied upon a belief that there existed discrete primordial races with fixed attributes. Moreover, although Vasconcelos often appears convinced that when these elements were blended together, 'whiteness', 'blackness' and so on, would disappear, and racial utopia would be achieved, he also considered that some racial elements were more desirable than others. Thus he argued that the input of 'inferior races' into the mixing process should be both limited and controlled. Indeed, there exists a telling slippage in Vasconcelos's work between the notions of 'mixture' and 'absorption'. As the passage below reveals, the latter process does not promise the destruction but rather the final victory of white racism.

> The lower types of the species will be absorbed by the superior type. In this manner, for example, the Black would be redeemed, and step by step, by voluntary extinction, the uglier stocks will give way to the more handsome. Inferior races, upon being educated, would become less prolific, and the better specimens would go on ascending a scale of ethnic improvement, whose maximum type is not precisely the White, but that new race to which the White himself will have to aspire with the object of conquering the synthesis.
>
> (1997, p. 32)

Vasconcelos's position provides a stark example of the way the celebration of racial hybridity can both challenge and affirm racism.

Tradition versus 'racism' in China

If we accept that race is a *modern* idea, elaborated in eighteenth- and nineteenth-century Europe as part and parcel of European science and global hegemony, it follows that a good place to look for opposition to the racialisation process is within traditional, *ante- or pre-modern*, practices and ideas. Indeed, the claim that European racism has been and is opposed by the egalitarianism of traditional culture, particularly religious culture, provides one of the focal points of anti-racist debate. The interaction of Islam and Western racism is, at the present time, the most well-known example of this discourse. The fact that, for reasons both religious and secular, certain Islamic societies resisted Western scientific racism has been substantiated by a number of historical researchers (for example, Majeed, 1997). However, it is misleading to conflate this history with the idea that Islam is necessarily anti-racist or that societies where Islam is the dominant religion are necessarily socially egalitarian or, indeed, have shunned ethnic or colour discrimination. As Lewis (1971) shows, colour consciousness and prejudice have been present within Middle Eastern Islamic cultures since the eighth century.

The positioning of Islamic tradition versus Western racism is, however, just one example of a much wider phenomenon. All over the world, including in the West itself, claims on older and/or more 'profound' cultural resources are frequently mobilised in the attempt to assert the 'otherness', the foreignness, and by implication the intrusive nature, of racism. Because this perspective represents a reaction to modern concerns and categories, the problems of historical interpretation inherent within such claims are usually overlooked. This is not simply a matter of noting that cultural traditions, such as religion, tend to have had diverse and flexible relations to racism. More fundamentally, it concerns the fact that pre-modern attitudes cannot be adequately understood in terms of contemporary preoccupations. The idea that being opposed to racial divisions and categories means that one is an egalitarian is a case in point. To us it may seem like a likely, almost commonsensical, connection. But it would not to many of those who are today regularly corralled into anti-racist history.

Although China provides many examples of radical, anti-traditional political projects, its history also contains one of the most important instances of the opposition of traditional thought to 'racism'. Such opposition involved the identification by scholars and other writers in nineteenth-century China schooled in established forms of social representation, of racial categories and racial thinking as a secular, alien and unwanted intrusion into their society. Racial thinking was opposed, not because it was anti-egalitarian, but because it threatened orthodox ways of understanding human difference. More precisely, 'racism' was considered part of a Western scientific, universalist world-view that downgraded the importance of the Chinese. For these conservative critics, racial science seemed to be suggesting that the Chinese, far from being at the centre of creation (the established, sinocentric, view), were just another people, to be studied and known, categorised and ranked, alongside the rest of humanity. Thus it was the fact that 'racism' seemed to augur a world of *human equivalence* that stirred the indignation and opposition of this group of critics.

The notion that there existed natural, biologically defined races whose attributes and possibilities were amenable to objective scientific enquiry became increasingly accepted in reform-minded intellectual circles in China from the late nineteenth century. This process reflected the increasing influence on China of Western science and socio-economic power. Those associated with adopting and adapting these ideas, such as Yan Fu (1853–1921), the writer who introduced Darwin and Spencer to a Chinese readership, and Pan Guangdan, who founded The Chinese Eugenics Institute in 1924, tended to be politically progressive. They wanted to sweep away the established order and create a 'rational' China (Dikötter, 1992). This period in Chinese history is sometimes termed 'the Chinese Enlightenment' (for example, Schwarcz, 1986). It is a provocative parallel. The phrase suggests that the assertion of rationality and universalism within Chinese society was a re-enactment of a European original. It is precisely such a narrative of 'progress', of 'development' simultaneously construed as modern, European and emancipatory, that helped justify the introduction of racist science into China. As this implies, the conservative opposition to this process was part of a wider defence of Chinese civilisation and the possibility of a distinct Chinese world-view.

The 'Scholars' Covenant', written in 1898, provided one of the clearest expressions of conservative opposition to racial thinking. It opposed the employment of 'foreign' terms, such as 'white race' and 'yellow race', and attempted to reaffirm a Chinese-centred vision of the world. As Dikötter explains: 'The traditional elite tried to maintain its power by discrediting the reformers' competing body of knowledge. For the conservatives, "race" was taboo, as it implied a degree of relativism that undermined the bases of their sinocentric universe' (1992, p. 95).

The ancient division between the Chinese centre and the barbarian, or foreign, margins was threatened by the racialisation process. The maintenance of traditional patterns of prejudice and hierarchy demanded that 'racism' be opposed. However, it would be a mistake to imagine that this mobilisation of 'traditional' thought merely represented the last gasp of a dying order. Although the reformers may be said to have obtained intellectual hegemony in the early twentieth century, 'traditional' notions continued to inform Chinese debates concerning human difference. Whether in the form of sinocentrism or within more particular *rapprochements* between Confucianism and racism, 'traditional' thinking continued to engage and challenge modern approaches. Thus, for example, an identification between the need for the preservation of 'the Chinese race' and the need to sustain 'the Confucian faith' developed from the beginning of the twentieth century, the latter providing an ethical and spiritual content to the otherwise overly mechanical presumptions of the former.

The example of conservative 'anti-racial' thinking in China finds many parallels around the world in situations where traditional social and religious dogma and Western racism have come into collision. However, as in China, the refutation of Western, secular racism has often been more to do with opposition to a modern, rationalist belief-system than any particular or unique disposition to social equality. Those inclined to celebrate 'traditional' non-racialised thinking as if it represents the existence of egalitarian cultural essences need to tread carefully; being opposed to racism does not necessarily mean that one believes everyone is equal.

Du Bois, racial soul and pan-Africanism

European claims of superiority, enforced and disseminated across the globe, have been resisted and refuted in many ways. However, within this history and geography certain tendencies have been established as paradigmatic, as representing the fundamentals of anti-racism. The assertion of loyalty to one's race, or 'race pride', is one such tendency. Such claims have been made in many different ways. However, they are more strongly associated with some oppressed groups than others. Indeed, for some commentators the notion of race pride appears to evoke the experience of one community in particular, African Americans. Any explanation of this association must take into account both the global influence upon twentieth-century culture of the USA and the formation of a diasporic black consciousness that is both constitutive of and resistant to white modernity (an argument developed by Gilroy, 1993). However we explain it, it is clear that certain African American thinkers and activists have been particularly influential in advancing the notion that the establishment of a sense of racial self-worth provides the most effective answer to white racism. And, if any name stands pre-eminent in this tradition, it is William Edward Burghardt Du Bois (1868–1963).

Du Bois is often read today as a precursor of more contemporary political and theoretical fashions and as a 'great man', a hero in the black 'hall of fame'. In his assessment of the way the name of Du Bois has come to be politically deployed Adolph Reed (1997, p. 4) notes a recurrent trend towards a 'hagiographical, sanitising impulse', a trend that undermines attempts to historically contextualise his work. Such approaches, Reed goes on to suggest, cannot adequately engage the way Du Bois's 'anti-racist' vision was animated by elitist and Eurocentric, as well as egalitarian, currents.

Du Bois's best-known written work is *The Souls of Black Folk*, published in 1903 (1989; see also Du Bois, 1968, 1985). It is a personal and autobiographical account of black life in white America, an account structured around the transcribed words and musical annotation of African American spirituals. However, the book's persistent return to the theme of racial sentiment has a highly analytical purport: to identify the way African Americans psychologically negotiate their way through the violence of white racism. This combination of narrative tones may be conveyed by reference to the opening passages of the book where Du Bois recounts the first time he felt himself being racially excluded.

> I remember well when the shadow swept across me. I was a little thing, away up in the hills of New England ... In a wee wooden schoolhouse, something put it into the boys' and girls' heads to buy gorgeous visiting-cards – ten cents a package – and exchange. The exchange was merry, till one girl, a tall newcomer, refused my card – refused it peremptorily, with a glance. Then it dawned upon me with a certain suddenness that I was different from others; or like, mayhap, in heart and life and longing, but shut out from their world by a vast veil.
>
> (1989, p.4)

This anecdote leads Du Bois to reflect on the construction of a 'Negro' identity that is both inside and outside American society. He identifies the resultant state of being as 'double-conscious-ness, this sense of always looking at one's self through the eyes of others, of measuring one's soul by the tape of a world that looks on in amused contempt and pity' (ibid., p. 5). *The Souls of Black Folk* represents one of the first sustained analyses of the psycho-logical impacts, the damage, of racism. Yet, far from locating these processes as parochially North American, Du Bois asserts that they are structuring dynamics of a global struggle for eman-cipation: 'The problem of the twentieth century is the color-line – the relation of the darker to the lighter races of men in Asia and Africa, in America and the islands of the sea' (ibid., p. 13).

Du Bois's scholarly work on the problem of racism carried on throughout his life. His most significant studies were historical reinterpretations of the role of African Americans in the shaping of the USA, reinterpretations that countered the academic ortho-doxy that black people were not to be taken seriously as political actors. *Black Reconstruction in America: 1860–1880* (1995, first published in 1935) represents Du Bois's weightiest statement of historical revisionism. The book chronicles the political possibili-ties both seized by and denied to African Americans within the period immediately after the American Civil War. Du Bois's concern to challenge traditional racist accounts of this period is particularly explicit in the book's closing chapter, titled 'The propaganda of history'. Here Du Bois surveys the existing historical literature, paying close attention to the kind of representations found with school text books. He identifies prevalent stereotypes, such as 'Negroes were responsible for bad government during Reconstruction' (ibid., p. 712) and 'All Negroes were lazy, dishonest and extravagant' (ibid., p. 711). Thus Du Bois advances a critical reading of existing histories, one that exposes their prejudices and explicitly claims for itself a greater regard for truth.

> Three-fourths of the testimony against the Negro in Reconstruction is on the unsupported evidence of men who hated and despised Negroes and regarded it as loyalty to blood, patriotism to country, and filial tribute to the fathers to lie, steal or kill in order to discredit these black folk ... what is inconceivable is that another generation and another group should regard this testimony as scientific fact, when it is contradicted by logic and by fact.
>
> (ibid., p. 725)

This passage suggests that Du Bois was not interested in offering or constructing an alternative, uniquely African American, version of reality but in challenging bias with objectivity. Extending this line of enquiry it may be argued that Du Bois's challenge to racism was expressed both within and against the Enlightenment traditions discussed earlier. On the one hand, Du Bois sought to affirm the folk content of African American culture and to suggest that black experience, most importantly the experience of 'double consciousness', provided a vantage point that offered insights unavailable from the insular, yet self-confidently universalist, perspective of white modernity. Yet, on the other hand, Du Bois was engaged in the ambitions of the Enlightenment. At a more general level Du Bois constantly affirmed that his work was part of Western intellectual history:

I sit with Shakespeare and he winces not. Across the color line I move arm in arm with Balzac and Dumas ... I summon Aristotle and Aurelius and what soul I will, and they come all graciously with no scorn nor condescension. So, wed with Truth I dwell above the Veil.

(1989, p. 90)

As with many intellectuals of the period, when Du Bois wished to secure an argument, he turned to science. Most importantly, Du Bois found in science the proof that racism was ill-founded. 'The leading scientists of the world have come forward', he wrote in 1911:

and laid down in categorical terms a series of propositions which may be summarized as follows:

1. (a)   It is not legitimate to argue from differences in phys-
          ical   characteristics   to   differences   in   mental
          characteristics ...
2. (b)   The civilization of a ... race at any particular moment
          of time offers no index to its innate or inherited capac-
          ities.

(cited by Appiah, 1986, p. 30)

Much of Du Bois's work evidences an intriguing ambivalence on the question of whether race is a real biological entity or a social experience (for discussion, see Logan, 1971; Appiah, 1986; Bell *et al.*, 1996). However, whatever his position on the scientific status of race, Du Bois's racial egalitarianism should not be confused with the abandonment of a Eurocentric view of civilisation and human development. Indeed, although often represented as a classic text of black affirmation, Du Bois makes it clear in *The Souls of Black Folk* that he regards African Americans as enthralled in a 'credulous race-childhood ... the sole oasis of simple faith and reverence in a dusty desert of dollars and smartness' (1989, p. 11). Du Bois looked forward, not to the disappearance of racial divisions, but to the recognition of different races' different 'traits and talents' in a nation where 'two world-races may give each other those characteristics both so sadly lack' (ibid., p. 11).

Du Bois's relationship to pan-Africanism was also influenced by his views on the meaning of civilisation. His anti-colonial message of 'Africa for the Africans' found expression at the five Pan-African Congresses he helped to organise (in 1919, 1921, 1923, 1927 and 1945). Yet it was a message with certain caveats: the 'principle of self-determination', Du Bois argued, 'cannot be wholly applied to semi-civilized peoples'. Such populations required 'the guidance of organized civilization', especially as represented by the 'twelve million civilized Negroes of the United States' (Du Bois, 1970, p. 273). As Reed (1997, p. 80) observes, Du Bois's vision relied on the deployment of an elite who 'represented within the African world the bearers of civiliza-tion and were to function as the carriers of the Enlightenment to Africa'.

Du Bois's version of pan-Africanism emerged alongside and to a certain extent in opposition to the more populist principles of the Universal Negro Improvement Association (UNIA). Founded in Jamaica in 1914 by Marcus Garvey, the UNIA was a mass movement (by 1923 it had over 6 million members in some 40 countries), which focused its efforts on enabling diasporic black communities to 'return' to Africa (Martin, 1983). Its influence on West Indian and African American cultural expression in the 1920s was also significant, Garveyism finding expression within the Harlem Renaissance and Rastafarianism (the latter being founded, among others, by ex-UNIA members in Jamaica in the early 1930s). The mass membership and appeal of such 'back to Africa' campaigning contrast sharply both with Du Bois's spurning of immigrationism as unrealistic and with the kind of people he wished to see lead the pan-African movement. The theme of leadership, more specifically of establishing a group of African leaders in waiting, animated the Pan-African Congresses Du Bois was involved in. Indeed, the 1945 Pan-African Congress, in Manchester, 'attracted the political and intellectual vanguard of the black world' (Marable, 1996, p. 211). Participants included Nkrumah, the first prime minister of an independent Ghana (from 1957) and Kenyatta, the first president of an independent Kenya (from 1963). For Du Bois the anti-colonial intent of pan-Africanism was never simply about 'deEuropeanising' Africa. It was also about modernising, civilising and leading Africa. The fact that the latter projects are so heavily laden with connotations of Europeanisation provides one of the key conundrums encountered by contemporary readers of Du Bois's work. However we define it, Du Bois clearly contributed significantly to 'the anti-racist tradition'. Yet Du Bois was a product of his times, a thinker who worked both in and against the Eurocentric assumptions of the early and mid-twentieth century.

Frantz Fanon: in and against the race concept

The status of the concept of race provides one of the key sites of controversy within contemporary anti-racism. In the aftermath of the Second World War, and the declarations of the United Nations (as discussed in Chapter 2), to oppose the division of the world into races and to assert the term's redundancy as a scientific form of classification, appeared to many to be the only viable anti-racist stance. Yet the fact that race is scientifically meaningless has not prevented oppression being carried out in its name. Thus, it may be argued, that the existence of racism creates the necessity for racialised resistance, for forms of ideology and solidarity constructed both by and against the racial categories imposed upon the world by the racist imagination. The difficulties and ambiguities of this position have encouraged an increasing appreciation of those activists from the past who simultaneously refused and deployed the race concept. The most influential and cited of such figures is Frantz Fanon.

Fanon was born in the French colony of Martinique in 1925. His writings on race and colonial liberation movements belong to a different generation than those previously addressed in this chapter. By the time his first book was published, *Black Skin, White Masks*, in 1952, many of the certainties of the Western Enlightenment had been undermined. The assumptions of

Vasconcelos and Du Bois, their willingness to situate themselves within a European tradition of egalitarian and philosophical effort, were, for Fanon, the subject of often agonising reflection and suspicion. Indeed, although there are many aspects to Fanon's work that bear comparison with Du Bois (Gaines, 1996), it is his insistent doubt, both about the value of the Enlightenment tradition and the nature of race, that most clearly testifies to his originality.

Fanon's was not a project of racial or cultural separatism, but of the examination of the social constitution of the racialised psyche. As this implies, Fanon had little time for the unthinking celebration of racial essences. 'The Negro is not', he wrote. 'Any more than the white man' (1986, p. 231). This phrase appears at the end of *Black Skin, White Masks* (1986). The meaning of Fanon's words becomes clearer in the context of the account earlier in the same volume of the author's own refusals of and dependencies upon racial identity. More precisely, Fanon attempts to locate, both emotionally and intellectually, the constitution of the colonised identity within and against white racism. '[W]hat is often called the black soul', notes Fanon, 'is a white man's artefact' (ibid., p. 16). 'It is the racist who creates his inferior' (ibid., p. 93). And yet, in order for racism to be resisted, in order for a post-colonial identity to be forged, the 'black soul' must be fabricated and asserted, given shape and definition as a site of resistance and revolution (Goldberg, 1996). Thus Fanon approached race-centred liberation movements with an uneasy mixture of derision and fascination. This is seen particularly clearly in his attitude to the black consciousness cultural movement known as negritude. The negritude poet Leopold Senghor's statement that 'Emotion is completely Negro as reason is Greek' was mocked by Fanon: 'Black magic, primitive mentality, animism, animal eroticism, it all floods over me', he jibes, 'I made myself the poet of the world' (1986, pp. 126–129). Extending his attack on both negritude, and those whites, such as Sartre, who sympathised with the negritude movement as a necessary moment in a more general emancipation (Sartre denoting negritude as 'anti-racist racism', cited by Fanon, ibid.,

p. 132), Fanon demands the right to both repudiate and create his own blackness. 'I tested the limits of my essence,' he says, 'beyond all doubt there was not much of it left' (ibid., p. 130). Searching for an original moment, a point that would 'shatter the hellish cycle' (ibid., p. 140), Fanon writes, 'I defined myself as an absolute intensity of beginning', a site of new possibilities, but also of violence and cathartic retreat from intellectualism: 'I took up my negritude and with tears in my eyes I put its machinery together again ... My cry grew more violent: I am a Negro, I am a Negro, I am a Negro ...' (ibid., p. 138).

Fanon's insistent reflexivity, his constant attempts to open up his own terminology and categories to inspection, made him aware of the difficulty of completely decolonising the radical imagination (see also Memmi, 1990). This struggle finds one of its clearest expressions in *The Wretched of the Earth* (1967; first published as *Les Damnes de la terre* in 1961), a book in which Sartre rather grandly claimed, 'the Third World finds *itself* and speaks to *itself* through [Fanon's] voice' (1967, p. 9). Here the hierarchical, exclusive content of Western 'tolerance' is vivisected, laid bare: 'the proclamation of an essential equality between men, manages to appear logical in its own eyes by inviting the sub-men to become human, and to take as their prototype Western humanity as incarnated in the Western bourgeoisie' (Fanon, 1967, p. 131).

Thus Fanon accuses the Enlightenment concept of universal 'Man' of being a device of colonial domination, a fraud that justifies exploitation. The urgency, and the hope, that inform the book derive from the conviction that such fraudulent ideologies of equality must and can be overturned through violent revolution.

Leave this Europe where they are never done talking of Man, yet murder men everywhere they find them, at the corner of every one of their own streets, in all the corners of the globe ... That same Europe where they never stopped proclaiming that they were only anxious for the welfare of Man: today we know with what sufferings humanity has paid for every one of their triumphs of the mind. Come, then, comrades, the European game has finally ended; we must find something different. We today can do everything, as long as we do not imitate Europe.

(ibid., pp. 251–252)

Yet Fanon's last rejoinder strikes a discordant note. The sense of infinite possibilities, of a complete severance from a European past, reflects more his role as revolutionary polemicist than anti-racist intellectual. It is a role that leads him to conclude *The Wretched of the Earth* with a utopian flourish, yet one that is, ironically, more firmly rooted in the mythologies of the Enlightenment than his less heroic pronouncements. 'It is a question', Fanon asserts, 'of the Third World starting a new history of Man ... we must work out new concepts, and try to set afoot a new man' (ibid., pp. 254–255).

The assertion that a post-racist identity entails the creation of a 'new man' is sustained in Sartre's (1967) introduction to *The Wretched of the Earth*. More specifically, Sartre casts European culture, and Europeans themselves, as deeply contaminated by racism. Addressing the book's European audience, he writes, 'You know well enough that we are exploiters' (ibid., p. 21), adding 'it would be better for you to be a native at the uttermost depths of his misery than to be a former settler' (ibid., p. 25). Mockingly, derisively, Sartre turns on the book's white readers – 'You, who are so liberal and so humane' (ibid., p. 12) – a gesture that, perhaps a little uneasily, collides the articulation of individual guilt and the critique of Western culture and capitalism. 'It is true, you are not settlers,' he writes, 'but you are no better' (ibid., p. 12). Thus Europeans too must make themselves anew. But, as the beneficiaries of racism, they cannot do this themselves, but must be violently, cathartically, defamiliarised with their own racism, a process that can be enabled by confrontation with their victims. 'Will we recover?', asks Sartre. 'Yes. For violence, like Achilles' lance, can heal the wounds that it has inflicted' (ibid., p. 25):

Europeans, you must open this book and enter into it. After a few steps in the darkness you will see strangers gathered around a fire; come close and listen, for they are talking of the destiny they will mete out to your trading-centres and to the hired soldiers who defend them. They will see you, perhaps, but they will go on talking among themselves, without even lowering their voices. This indifference strikes home; their fathers, shadowy creatures, *your* creatures, were but dead souls; you it was who allowed them glimpses of light ... Now, at a respectful distance, it is you who feel furtive, nightbound and perished with cold ... Our victims know us by their scars and by their chains and it is this that makes their evidence irrefutable.

(Sartre, 1967, pp. 11–12)

Sartre's reading of Fanon cements some of the less reflexive trajectories apparent in the latter's work. The agonising fluidity so apparent in *White Skins, Black Masks* is fashioned into new, easily comprehensible subject positions, namely the angry black victim and the guilty white racist. These devices reflect Fanon's and Sartre's role as active political participants in anti-racist, anti-colonial struggles. Neither man saw himself simply as a theorist, a thinker wishing to explore 'complexity'. In both cases the strategic necessity of forming and defending fixed, political identities formed a tense yet creative relationship with less certain, more fluid, speculations on the way that 'The Negro is not. Any more than the white man'.

I would emphasise again that the four case studies presented here are not designed to provide an overview of the entire field of non-European opposition to racism. Indeed, the ideological diversity evidenced by my examples should warn against such an endeavour. The roots of anti-racism reach away in many different directions, branching and tangling with myriad traditions. They certainly cannot be potted neatly into sentimental cliché: resistance and struggle are part of the pre-history of anti-racism but so are complicity and conservatism. Just as unsettling within the preceding narratives lies the gnawing sense that the act of abstracting 'non-European' traditions of anti-discrimination into a discrete sub-heading is both necessary and fraudulent. European racism, as Fanon argued, necessitates identities of oppression and resistance. The 'non-European', like the 'European', has been brought into being, given shape and social consequence. Such categories cannot be wished away, for they are integral to the ideological structuring of the world around us. Moreover, Fanon's formulation is itself only a partial view of this relationship. It fails to engage those traditions of interpretation that both reproduce and invent forms of identity that are not dependent upon European power. Chinese, African, and Latin American identities simultaneously evidence, interrogate and escape European racialisations. It is true that Europeans tried to impose their ideologies and categories upon the rest of the world's populations. An important question for anti-racists is how far they have been successful.

CONCLUSION

This chapter has sought to show the diverse sources that may be identified as feeding into modern anti-racisms. I have tried to show that these roots run deep into history and stretch right across the globe. I have also attempted to exemplify the fact that racism and anti-racism are not necessarily two discrete warring discourses, good versus evil. A more uncomfortable but also, I believe, more truthful and useful approach has been attempted, one that shows the ambiguities within the politics of 'anti-racism'. As we have seen, the 'anti-racist' and the 'racist' are very often the same person; the individual who struggles against racial intolerance and discrimination may also be someone who believes in racial and/or social hierarchy and the superiority of the West.

It is a testament to the inadequacy of contemporary debate on anti-racism that much of the material introduced here will be new to many readers. Paul Gilroy (1993, p. 90), writing about Britain, notes the existence of a 'beleaguered contemporary anti-racism which is struggling to find precedents and to escape the strictures of its own apparent novelty'. It is, indeed, a burden to imagine that opposition to racial discrimination is new. Even more oppressive, perhaps, is the notion that anti-racist opposition

is necessarily of one sort, arising from one source, from one political tradition.

2

CLAIMING EQUALITY

Nations, capitalism and anti-racism

INTRODUCTION

Anti-racism is routinely posited as a spirit of defiance, a product of individual or collective oppositional will. This association is, however, based on a very narrow view of anti-racism's relationship to modernity. For anti-racism is not merely about resistance. It is also about the creation of sustainable states, the reproduction of modern economies and the establishment of internationally accepted principles of political legitimacy. After the Second World War something approaching a consensus was established among Western nations that racism was unacceptable; that legitimate forms of political or economic governance could not be seen to condone racial inequality. This perspective found institutional expression in a variety of international initiatives. 'There is', noted one senior British official in the wake of the clear opposition to race discrimination offered in the United Nations Charter (1945), 'something like official unanimity of opposition to this species of primitive prejudice' (Corbett, quoted by Füredi, 1998,

p. 13). Today the corporate sector in many countries also partici-
pates in the rhetoric of racial tolerance. The notion that
multinational capitalism is perforce multicultural capitalism, and
that 'diversity' and 'equal opportunities' provide 'resources' to be
developed and tapped, have become familiar themes within business management.

Two questions arise from this state of affairs. First, why and
how has anti-racism developed within and through modern forms
of political and economic control over territory and capital?
Second, given the claimed complicity between these interests and
anti-racism, why is the latter so often represented as a form of
radicalism, a subversion of the established order? Since many of
the issues that cluster round the radical image of anti-racism are
addressed elsewhere in this book, this chapter will be concen-
trating on the first of these questions, exploring the nature and
limits of the relationship between anti-racism, national and international identity and capitalism. In fact, as we shall see, a clue to
the answer of the second question emerges from these considerations, namely the hollowness of many of the claims to anti-racism
made by nationalists and capitalists. It would be misleading,
however, to give the impression that these claims are equally or,
indeed, necessarily insubstantive. This chapter shows that nationalism and capitalism have provided certain important spaces for
anti-racism but that the forms they enable or permit tend to be of
a highly circumscribed kind. More specifically, the rhetoric of
racial tolerance has been used to incorporate and assimilate populations into national and/or capitalist ambitions. Anti-racism has
come to be employed as a component of national identity, a
symbol of the benefits of national allegiance, and as a way of
dismantling forms of prejudice that militate against the mobility
of labour and capital. These forms of anti-racism are often of far
more consequence than popular and agitational movements.
Nevertheless, they are nearly always, in part, provoked by such
activism. In other words, the anti-racism of the powerful tends to
be initiated by factors that are not completely in their control,
most importantly the pressure for change exerted by the struggles
of oppressed groups.

NATIONAL AND INTERNATIONAL CLAIMS TO ANTI-RACISM

Opposition to racism has become a familiar element within the rhetorical repertoires of governments. Anti-racism is both laid claim to and a site of, sometimes, intense rivalry. Indeed, during the Cold War one of the most sensitive areas in US politics was the comparison of American racism and Soviet, and, by extension, communist, racial tolerance. It bears repeating that the concept of 'racism' was first formulated, and remains most ubiquitously employed, as an accusation. It is something to be denied in oneself and to charge others with. The second half of the twentieth century saw this negative association become increasingly cemented into discourses of national and international political legitimacy. Anti-racism became an ideological arena where governments and other powerful institutions can prove themselves worthy of power.

Government rhetoric in this area tends to invoke cynicism among activists who often find it difficult to make politicians translate their words and their legal obligations into reality. However, it is also worth considering the way the tasks performed by modern states encourage such displays of racial egalitarianism. It is, first of all, useful to recall that the concept of the nation-state was, in part, developed in opposition to the exclusionary collectivities of the pre-modern period. As Hobsbawm (1992, p. 33) notes, the process of 'liberal nation-making' in the eighteenth century sought to unify disparate populations within politically defined states, a process that 'was evidently incompatible with definitions of nations as based on ethnicity, language or common history'. This implies that, although pluralism may present a dilemma for modern states (see Bullivant, 1981), the latter provide a potential space for the acceptance of diversity. This tendency within the nation-building process implies that the normative unit of the 'authentically modern' nation-state is the citizen, and that citizens participate in society as legal equals. Extending this line of thought we might even be tempted to suggest that nations that 'give into' *volkish* or other ethnically exclusionary projects are inauthentic and atavistic. However, this would be to concede to a comforting delusion: the history of modern nations suggests that exclusionary and inclusionary, racist and anti-racist, tendencies co-exist within modernity, that modernity both produces and repudiates ethnocentrism (Bonnett, 1999). Modern history would also suggest that the model of the politically defined citizen is more important for its role as a legitimising ideal than for its accuracy as a representation of reality. Indeed, the fact that this ideal is also a model of incorporation, that claims of inclusion are always also justifications of nation building, provides perhaps the best explanation of why 'many peoples, one nation' has become a politicians' cliché employed around the globe.

The assimilative function of anti-racism becomes most explicit when race equity initiatives are introduced as a means of resolving racialised conflicts deemed to be posing a threat to the integrity of the nation. Indeed, many of the most far-reaching anti-racist policies take the form of national 'salvation plans'. The practice of positive discrimination in Malaysia is a case in point. This policy, one of the most ambitious of its kind in the world, has involved the promotion of indigenous Malay interests and control in the spheres of land distribution, employment, education and taxation. The New Economic Policy (NEP) that introduced affirmative action in Malaysia was put in place following a 'race riot' on 13 May 1969 in Kuala Lumpur between Malays and Chinese, a riot which left some 200 people dead (Comber, 1988). As expressed within the Second Malaysia Plan, the NEP was designed to 'accelerate the process of restructuring Malaysian society to correct economic imbalance, so as to reduce and eventually eliminate the identification of race with economic function' (Government of Malaysia, 1971, p. 1). The NEP set a quota of 40 per cent Malay employment for most industries and a target of 30 per cent Malay ownership of commercial and industrial activities. A parallel measure, the Constitution (Amendment) Bill, gave powers to the government to direct universities to lower their qualification entrance requirements for Malay students. There remains a debate about the utility of the

NEP for the development of capitalism in Malaysia (Jesudason, 1989; Chowdhury and Islam, 1996). However, Prime Minister Mahathir, one of the architects of the NEP, was in no doubt about the affinity of interest of nation, capital and racial equity. The NEP's 'formulation', he explained, 'was made necessary by the economic needs of the nation as much as its socio-political needs. There can be no economic stability without political stability and social stability. Thus the NEP is also a formula for economic growth' (1976).

NATIONAL TRADITIONS OF ANTI-RACISM?

Opposition to racial oppression has long been formulated as a national boast. Indeed, there are few countries where a tradition of racial tolerance is not employed in this manner. It is worth recalling that even at the height of its imperial endeavours, it was common for British politicians to aver to that country's proud record in the struggle against racial injustice. 'The unwearied, unostentatious, and inglorious crusade of England against slavery', noted the Victorian historian William Lecky (1869, p. 169), 'may probably be regarded as among the three or four perfectly virtuous acts accorded in the history of nations.' Across the English Channel similar claims were heard. Indeed, the maxim 'There are no slaves in France' appears to have been current from the sixteenth century (Peabody, 1996). The latter contention found an echo in 1973 in President Pompidou's (cited by Lloyd, 1998, p. 1) assertion that 'France is profoundly anti-racist.' Such invocations of a public heritage of racial equality represent a form of national myth-making. The need to assert such a legacy is, however, contingent upon both political pressures (for example, it is noteworthy that Pompidou's claim came only in the wake of several racist murders in France) as well as the ideological arrogations of the state. With respect to the latter it is pertinent to consider the fact that the most trenchant national claims to anti-racism emerged from communist states. Within the USSR, the principle of the equality of the races, included in the Soviet Constitution of 1918, was soon deemed to have been achieved in practice. The eradication of racism was offered as both a national vindication of the Soviet Union and as a testament of the benefits of communism. As this implies, the maintenance of this clause in the 1977 Constitution of the USSR (Article 36 proclaimed that 'any advocacy of racial or national exclusiveness, hostility or contempt, [is] punishable by law') was an act of largely symbolic significance. In fact, since racism was identified as a problem of capitalism, the issue was rarely taken seriously: far from being eradicated, racism in the USSR was ignored or recategorised. It is one of the telling historical ironies of national anti-racism that the collapse of many of those governments who proclaimed their territories most free of racism (that is, the communist regimes of Eastern and Middle Europe) was followed by both the exposure and rapid development of racist movements.

Where grass-roots pressure against racial discrimination has arisen within state communism it has often been considered with extreme suspicion by the authorities. Even in Cuba, where the black majority gave its overwhelming support for the 1959 socialist revolution at least in part because it was assumed it would challenge racism, Afro-Cuban groups trying to assert an independent anti-racist trajectory have been cast by the state as counter-revolutionary and suppressed. Indeed, in recent years, the assertion of 'multiculturalism' within contemporary Cuba has been aligned, not with state socialism, but with the need to encourage tourism. McGarrity and Cárdenas (1995) report that

> Religions of African origin that were viewed as manifestations of superstition, backwardness and irrationality have been elevated to the status of reflections of Cuba's 'exotic' Caribbean culture. The reason may lie in official recognition that tourists have to be provided with 'local culture' to consume.
>
> (ibid., p. 102)

At this juncture it may be useful to ask a basic question: in what sense is the notion of a 'national anti-racist tradition' either accurate or useful? In the context of the parochial nature of much English-language debate, the notion of 'national anti-racist traditions' clearly has some utility in alerting us to the existence of different cultures of race equality. However, it is also appropriate to place such a phrase, at least mentally, in scare quotes. For if employed dogmatically the notion of 'national traditions' in this area can homogenise diverse societies, overlook local differences and reduce the story of anti-racism to national narratives, with national actors forging discrete national identities. Such a portrayal can easily slip into precisely the kind of self-vindicating rhetoric of glorious and successful 'anti-racist traditions' favoured by nationalists. Other methodological problems that surround this issue have been identified as 'the two models fallacy' and 'definitional dilemmas'. The former appellation comes from Silverman (1992) and Lloyd (1993a) who have both commented on the poverty of interpreting French and 'Anglo-Saxon' attitudes to anti-racism as if they represented two pure and opposing models. Lloyd (1993a) argues that 'The construction of two imaginary models, counterposed to one another in a positive/negative binary opposition, should alert us to the presence of a polemic. The dualistic form obscures the complexities of difference.' A second potential problem for national comparisons relates to differences in language and definition. Again, Lloyd (1993b, p. 259) provides a valuable warning. Terminological differences, she notes, can

> reflect more fundamental differences in the way in which people think of relationships, or in the basic approach to nation and race. What do the French really mean when they speak of 'immigrants' and the Germans 'Ausländer'? This can only really make sense when seen within the broader context of the social relationship (of migrant worker/settler and receiving society).
>
> (ibid.)

As this implies, anti-racism needs to be understood as working on multiple levels, and within various forms of discourse. It has a national and government voice. But it also has populist voices, propagandist voices, conservative voices, revolutionary voices, transnational voices, and so on. Anti-racism cannot be exhausted, or adequately summed up, by simply mining any one of these seams and affixing a national label to one's endeavours. As this implies, essays with titles such as 'Australian anti-racism' or 'French anti-racism' need to be approached with circumspection. Such terms are better approached as *claims* than as descriptions.

An attendant problem with analyses that suggest there are discrete national traditions of anti-racism is that they tend to overlook the international currents, and influences, within anti-racist theory and practice. The effect anti-racist ideas and categories understood to have been developed within the twentieth-century's principal world power, the USA, have had on other societies' equity discourses provides the most important example of this phenomenon. The adoption and adaptation of the binary system of racial categorisation often associated with the USA, i.e. dividing people into blacks or whites, may be seen today in many countries around the world. The symbolic power and utility of American models and images of racial conflict and identity have enabled British Asians, German Turks, Japanese Ainu, Australian Aborigines and many other groups to draw on an increasingly well-known repertoire of global clichés of racial rebellion and resistance. Commentating on this process in Britain, Hiro (1971) quotes a remark made by one British Asian youth in the late 1960s in the context of a rising tide of racial attacks: 'I'm black and I'm beautiful.' It is a statement that resonates with both the politics of resistance and of the insertion of African American blackness, and, by implication, European American whiteness, as archetypal positions within British racial politics.

Yet although discussing 'national traditions' of anti-racism is a hazardous undertaking, the fact remains that particular anti-racisms can often be much better understood once placed in the context of the attitudes towards racial and ethnic inequality prevalent within their 'country of origin'. Moreover, the majority of anti-racist groups are either nationally organised, or locally based contributions to a wider national anti-racist effort. I shall use two examples to illustrate why it can be useful to interrogate both the nationality of and the nationalism within anti-racism: France and Canada. Both countries have relatively well-developed anti-racist state polices and popular movements. However, the articulation of these traditions in each country reflects a number of interesting differences. Crudely expressed, the assimilationist dynamic that coheres both 'traditions' has tended to be framed in terms of the affirmation of a multicultural or 'mosaic' society in Canada and in terms of a unified and unifying egalitarian society and state in France.

'French anti-racism'

That there is such a thing as 'French anti-racism', i.e. a form of anti-racism that is rooted in French society and is part of a French tradition, is generally taken for granted within debates on racism in France. In *Discourses of Antiracism in France* Catherine Lloyd (1998) explains that it is a tradition that is often claimed to reach back to Renaissance and Enlightenment thinkers, a tradition that reflects both a moral and intellectual commitment within French society to social equality. Moreover, this narrative is asserted with almost equal vigour by non-governmental as by governmental anti-racist organisations. The President of the independent Mouvement Contre le Racisme, l'Anti-Sémitisme et Pour la Paix (MRAP) noted in 1957 that 'Anti-racism ... reflects a glorious French tradition, affirmed throughout our history from Montaigne, to the Abbé Grégoire, from Schelcher to Zola, finding its expression in our immortal Declaration of the Rights of Man and of the Citizen' (Caen, cited by Lloyd, 1998, p. 62. Founded in 1949, the MRAP united the Mouvement National contre le Racisme and Union des Juifs pour la Résistance et l'Entre'aide. It remains the largest and most influential of the French anti-racist groups). Such assertions reflect a continuing faith in a vision of the French Revolution as the defining moment in the politics of social equality. In 1985 the MRAP's journal *Différences* reaffirmed this conviction:

> By founding 'French antiracism' the Republic repelled the backward looking who rejected the tremendous upheavals through which Toussaint l'Ouverture entered into French history ... The anti-racist achievement of the Revolution amounted to a massive naturalisation. Jews, protestants, black slaves of the colonies, all entered the community of citizens in the name of the universal principles of Reason and Right.
>
> With the Republic, anyone can join the nation, whether catholic, protestant or jew, white or black, rich or poor, by simply adhering to the project of Liberty and Equality.
>
> (*Différences*, cited by Lloyd, 1998, p. 57)

As this statement implies, the assimilation of minorities into French culture has not traditionally been interpreted as a conservative project but as part of the emancipatory logic of egalitarianism. It is a project, moreover, that has been applied not merely to immigrants and their descendants but to the various regional cultures within France (see Safran, 1984). Hence, social equality is seen to be achieved through 'entry' into the universally valid ideals of the French Revolution, a perspective that establishes France as the progenitor, arbiter and authentic home of anti-racism. Where other forms of agency are recognised, they are co-opted into this narrative (note the reference in the passage from *Différences* cited above to how Toussaint l'Ouverture 'entered into French history'). Thus, struggles against slavery by slaves, or against anti-Semitism by Jews, are represented as attempts to access French enlightenment. 'Frenchness', constructed in this way, is always politically 'in front' of such movements, extending a welcoming hand back to help them 'on board'. Those forms of anti-racism that this discourse of national identity cannot easily assimilate tend to be marginalised. More specifically, both the failure of the putative forefathers of French anti-racism always to obey the protocols of the contemporary movement and the fact that 'the French tradition' only came into being because it was forced on to the political agenda in France by those fighting against French domination, have tended to be overlooked. In the remainder of this section I shall develop each of these two themes.

'Everyone', it was noted in *Différences* in 1989, 'now recognises Grégoire as one of the fathers of modern antiracism' (cited by Lloyd, 1998, p. 42). In fact, a consideration of the anti-slavery activism of the French clergyman and revolutionary Abbé Henri Grégoire (1750–1831) provides a useful insight into some of the principal tensions and blindspots within 'the French tradition'. The Abbé was tireless in his assertion of universal human equality. A member of the first French abolitionist group, the *Société des Amis des Noirs* (founded 1789), Grégoire noted that black people

> being the same nature as the whites, have the same rights as they to exercise and the same duties to fulfil ... we may say, in general, that virtue and vice, wisdom and foolishness, genius and stupidity, belong to all countries, nations, heads and complexions.
>
> (cited by Aptheker, 1993, p. 109)

As part of his agitational work Grégoire provided an essay prize on the topic 'What is the best way to erase the white man's unjust and barbaric prejudice against African and mulatto skin colour?'. Grégoire's opinions were not, however, always so uniform with contemporary anti-racist principles. More specifically, his belief in a model of 'Man' based on an enlightened French original led him to assert that slaves were not yet ready for freedom. Indeed, when slavery was abolished by the revolutionary French government, on the 16th Pluviose of the Year 2 of the French Republic (4 February 1794), the Abbé was appalled. He claimed, writes Lloyd (1994, p. 240), 'that suddenly to emancipate black slaves was equivalent to beating a pregnant woman so that she could give premature birth'. As this implies, while Grégoire was an important figure in asserting the issue of racial equality in France, the act of abolition itself had other causes.

Chief among these was the revolt of the slaves themselves. Indeed, there exists an instructive relationship between the French Revolution and black revolt. Each catalysed the other to produce abolition. Many of the black rebel leaders in the colony that did most to force the French government's hand on the issue, San Domingo (Haiti), understood themselves as part of the Enlightenment project. A series of uprisings in San Domingo between 1790 and 1791, sparked, at least in part, by the French Revolution, thrust the issue of slavery onto the agenda of the revolutionary Convention in Paris. In *The Black Jacobins* (1994) C.L.R. James discusses the sympathy of interests between the two groups of revolutionaries. James also makes it clear that the French Convention was forced into abolition; that it was not French altruism that produced emancipation but rebellion. Once news of the decision by the Convention to abolish slavery reached San Domingo, it encouraged many rebels to align themselves with the French Republic. 'To all the blacks', writes James, 'revolutionary France, which had decreed equality and the abolition of slavery, was a beacon among the nations' (1994, p. 231). Yet the subsequent restoration of slavery in French colonies by Napoleon Bonaparte is testament to the fragility of the emancipatory impetus in France. In San Domingo itself, however, the revolt was carried forward. A successful war of independence was fought with France and an independent Republic of Haiti was proclaimed on 1 January 1804.

The notion of an endogenous French anti-racism is equally difficult to sustain within the twentieth century. Anti-colonial agitation and the struggles of racialised immigrants to France have continuously provoked and sustained 'French anti-racism'. The war of independence in Algeria provides a case in point. During the 1950s mounting evidence of French atrocities in Algeria forced the issue of colonialism onto the agenda of anti-racist organisations in France. Thus, for example, after revelations of torture by the French military, the MRAP, shifting its rhetoric away from an advocacy of the universal benefits of association with France, began to support Algerian independence.

Nevertheless, anti-colonialism remains a difficult issue within a movement that can still appear committed to a normative and prescriptive model of the French Enlightenment. Indeed, a reflection of the remaining unease about denouncing French colonialism may be detected in the way that, from the early 1960s, the MRAP and other anti-racist groups turned increasingly away from international concerns and towards campaigning on experiences of racism in France. More specifically, racial violence and the economic marginalisation of immigrants from North Africa and the French Caribbean became key sites of activism. It is important to note, however, that while France was engaged in imperial warfare such concerns could never be satisfactorily severed from the colonial struggle. It is even more pertinent to recall that the worst single act of racist violence in France during the 1960s was the massacre of between 200 and 400 supporters of Algerian independence by French police in Paris on 17 October 1961.

Once racism in France had been established as the legitimate focus of 'French anti-racism', the issue of anti-racist legislation gained increasing prominence within the movement. One of the successes of the MRAP, in association with the Ligue contre l'Antisémitisme et le Racisme (founded 1928), was to lobby the French government to introduce the 1972 Law Against Racism (see Costa-Lascoux, 1994). Although Article 2 of the 1958 French Constitution claims to ensure 'equality of citizens ... without distinction' of 'race' it was widely held to be ineffective, a specific law against racism being seen as a way of highlighting and targeting the issue. The law, which implemented obligations under the United Nations' International Convention on the Elimination of All Forms of Racial Discrimination, has two parts, the first outlawing racist utterances or writings, the second outlawing acts of racial discrimination. The low level of prosecution under the law testifies, however, to the fact that the onus of proof on the prosecution has tended to be unrealistically high.

In the early 1980s the experience of prejudice in France was consolidated as a focus of activism by the emergence of a new, youth-oriented, anti-racist agenda. In 1983 a *Marche pour l'Egalité* travelled through numerous cities and suburbs of France, providing a forum for solidarity for young people of North African and Caribbean heritage. The emphasis on the post-colonial identities and experiences of racism of this group was integrated by a new organisation, SOS-Racisme (founded in 1984), into popularist campaigning directed against the influence of the far-right Front Nationale. Using music festivals and advertising campaigns SOS-Racisme attempted to combat xeno-phobic and anti-immigrant sentiment by propounding a familiar vision of France's heritage of tolerance and equality. As one of the group's leaders, Halem Désir, noted, 'our only ideological reference is the Rights of Man' (cited by Lloyd, 1998, p. 221).

However, the tendency of groups such as SOS-Racisme to evoke the issue of identity as a key site of activism inevitably threatens the claims to universalism characteristic of the French anti-racist tradition. This trend is sometimes construed as representing the intrusion of foreign, more specifically American, ideas into the national debate. It is pertinent to mention here that within France 'the French approach' to anti-racism is often contrasted with the so-called 'Anglo-Saxon' model supposedly applied in the USA (and, to a lesser extent, Britain). Within the latter societies, it is suggested, a relativist paradigm dominates anti-racism, with considerable attention being given to the preservation and celebration of racial difference and, by extension, to the race concept itself. This approach is compared to the French assertion of universal rights and freedoms, and to a secular, rational, tradition of equality in which racial differences are denied scientific or political credibility. Thus, for example, the French government's *Haut Conseil à l'Intégration* opined that

> [the] French conception of integration should obey a logic of equality and not a logic of minorities. The principles of identity and equality which go back to the Revolution and the Declaration of the Rights of Man and of Citizens impregnate our conception, thus founded on the equality of individuals before the law, whatever their origin, race, religion ... to the exclusion of an institutional recognition of minorities.
>
> (cited by Lloyd, 1991, p. 65)

However, although assimilationist attitudes form the intellectual inheritance of contemporary French anti-racism, they are increasingly being called into question. In part as a consequence of the assertion of regional ethnic identities within France in the 1960s, as well as the anti-authoritarian, cultural politics of groups like SOS-Racisme, both new and established French anti-racist groups now appear to be trying to balance relativism and universalism. Thus, for example, the Mouvement Contre le Racisme, l'Anti-Sémitisme et Pour la Paix changed its name in 1980 to Mouvement Contre le Racisme, et Pour l'Amitié entre les Peuples and adopted the slogan 'equally in difference'. The new President of the organisation noted: 'Each culture brings to the human symphony, sonorities and harmonies proper to itself. In praising difference, we should see not an appeal for separation and ignorance but an appeal for exchange, dialogue and fraternity' (cited by Lloyd, 1994, p. 226). This trend provides a clear challenge to the notion that there exists a coherent, discrete tradition of 'French anti-racism'. And, perhaps, by reconceptualising and reinventing the history of 'French anti-racism' it may be possible to assimilate 'pluralism' within a new national discourse. However, as we shall see, there are other countries well ahead of France in positing diversity as a core national attribute.

'Canadian anti-racism'

In marked contrast to the relatively centralised and assimilationist French state, Canada is a politically devolved society, where both the majority of federal and provincial governments claim to accommodate and celebrate ethnic and racial pluralism. Indeed, according to Adam (1992, p. 22), pluralism in Canada is now 'built into the national consciousness'. Canadian federal policies on race and ethnicity, Adam continues, in comparison with those in many European countries, are predicated upon a 'weak notion of national identity that does not encourage a self-confident "host" group to impose its cultural definitions on the rest' (ibid., p. 22). It should also be added that Canadian initiatives in this area do not tend to rely on an historical reading of Canada as possessing a long history of, or unique claim to, egalitarianism. Rather, notions of 'Canadian anti-racism' and 'Canadian multi-culturalism' tend to be seen as representing contemporary solutions to contemporary dilemmas. The earliest articulations of a 'Canadian approach' concerned the management of the division between Anglophone and Francophone Canada through federal and provincial policies of bi-lingualism. However, the impact of immigration from other European and non-European countries, as well as the assertion of native Canadian rights and cultures, placed considerable pressure on this binary model of Canadian society. Thus, Prime Minister Pierre Trudeau's adoption of multi-culturalism as a national ideology in 1971, although initially designed to respond to the concerns of white ethnic minorities in the mid-West, considerably extended the parameters of Canadian pluralism. '[A]lthough there are two official languages there is no official culture', noted Trudeau (1971, p. 1), 'nor does any ethnic group take precedence over any other'. The initial objections to multiculturalism came largely from the Francophone community who believed that such a policy might undermine their status as a core constituent of the Canadian nation. As Edwards (1992, p. 25) points out, 'a cynical view holds that the greater support from the English sector [for multiculturalism] exists because it is seen as a defusing of the French "problem" in Canada'. Other commentators, such as Moodley (1992, p. 79), have suggested that the official endorsement of multiculturalism at the federal level not only provided the state with a means of responding to 'the impasse between French-speakers in Quebec and the English provinces' but also offered a way of dealing with pressures from First Nation Canadians and 'immigrant minorities'. Thus, she argues, the adoption of a multicultural policy was 'firmly linked with political hegemony':

> By formally acknowledging the varieties of cultural adherence in the Canadian mosaic, the existing cultural hierarchy was in no way threatened but stabilised by diffusion of claims of infe-riority with pluralism. Conservative as well as social democratic administrations have subsequently embraced the

policy with equal enthusiasm. The Canadian mosaic was elevated to a national consensus and official ideology while *de facto* membership in the charter cultures continued to determine life chances.

(ibid., p. 79)

Reflecting the conviction that the affirmation of diversity acts as a kind of ideological glue keeping the country together, multiculturalism has, as Moodley notes, achieved acceptance within the mainstream of Canadian political life. Indeed, one commentator felt able to write in 1989 that

The policy is generously funded ... and the premises of the program – the support of the separate and linguistic identity of different ethnic groups, including recent minorities – is supported by all the major parties, and all provincial governments. Multiculturalism's critics are rarely heard in the public arena.

(Bagley, 1989, p. 101)

The fact that Canadian race equity initiatives often represent an attempt to assimilate all Canadians into, as well as to create, a national identity has not been lost on some of those within native Canadian communities. As the increasing use of the designation 'First Nations' for native Canadians implies, certain indigenous voices have been attempting to develop their own national identity, an identity that is not merely a sub-set of 'Canadian'. Indeed, one government equity consultant in British Columbia explained to me in 1996 (see Carrington and Bonnett, 1997) that many First Nation people in the province had disassociated themselves from the race equality movement. He suggested that this phenomenon represented a form of resistance:

They realise that [they] would be co-opted in your game. Because the anti-racist movement is really trying to integrate [them] into the system ... Well [they are] saying no, 'I want to be treated as an equal partner, and more than that, a separate nation state'.

The messages on a series of posters issued by the Government of British Columbia in the mid-1990s, and displayed on buses and other public places, provide an insight into the rationale behind such fears: 'Multiculturalism is a united Canada'; 'Mutual respect unites Canada'; 'Working together brings prosperity'. A logic of national co-existence animates such slogans, a logic that suggests that an ethnic group's commitment to the nation is dependent upon, and should arise from, the knowledge that its distinctiveness will be respected within that society.

In France, where a strong and unified national identity is assumed, cultural diversity has often been understood as a threat to national identity. Similar fears have been expressed in other countries in Europe as well as within the USA. In Canada, by contrast, where a 'weak' or diffuse notion of national identity is widely accepted, multiculturalism has blossomed and come to represent one of the defining, and hence integrating, aspects of Canadian life and values. Moreover, in the 1980s and 1990s, the devolution of power in Canada enabled some provincial governments, dominated by the left-wing New Democratic Party (NDP), to combine multiculturalism with a more explicit opposition to racism. This process led to 'anti-racism' being posited as a critique of multiculturalism and as a form of radical challenge to entrenched racism in Canadian society. The most significant examples of this tendency were the anti-racist initiatives developed within Ontario in the mid-1990s. Although various interest groups had lobbied for this development, it was the demands and activism of African Canadians that were perceived as providing the key catalyst. This association was particularly apparent in the Ontario Government's justification of its anti-racist policies in 1992, policies introduced in the wake of riots in Toronto widely construed as being 'black led' and symptomatic of African Canadian alienation and disaffection. For example, the former NDP leader, Stephen Lewis – who was asked by the provincial premier to 'consult widely' and make policy recommendations in the light of these disturbances – was clear in his appraisal both that the riots resulted from the grievances of 'black youth' and that African Canadians were the primary victims of racism in Toronto. In his report Lewis noted that

> what we are dealing with at root, and fundamentally, is anti-black racism. While it is obviously true that every visible minority community experiences the indignities and wounds of systematic discrimination throughout Southern Ontario, it is the Black community which is the focus. It is Blacks who are being shot, it is black youth that is unemployed in excessive numbers, it is black students who are inappropriately streamed in schools, it is black kids who are disproportionately dropping-out ... Just as the soothing balm of 'multiculturalism' cannot mask racism, so racism cannot mask its primary target.
>
> (1992)

The attempt to construct anti-racism as an oppositional tradition has not, however, proved to be sustainable either federally or at a provincial level. More specifically, the political connotations of formulating anti-racism in this way and aligning it with the NDP broke with the political consensus surrounding ethnic pluralism, making this new form of anti-racism vulnerable to accusations of left-wing bias (indeed, subsequent to the Conservative defeat of the NDP in Ontario in 1995, many of their anti-racist initiatives were disbanded). As this suggests, national traditions of anti-racism tend to rely on broad-based political support. The sustainability of such discourses depends on the invisibility of their politics, on the presumption that there is some natural link between 'the people' and the nation. The attacks on 'left-wing anti-racism' did little to dislodge the pluralist, multicultural model of 'Canadian anti-racism' precisely because the latter has come to articulate and cohere national identity.

The examples of France and Canada are illustrative of two countries with distinctive claims on anti-racism. Within France the assumption of the universal status and relevance of French notions of liberty and equality – an assumption heavily reliant on the deployment of French history – has animated the debate. With Canada, by contrast, a vision of national integration occurring through the contemporary acceptance of ethnic diversity dominates debate. Yet both articulations of anti-racism remain, at root, assimilationist in their intent and implications. Each offers racial equality as both a reward for and a defining feature of membership of the national unit.

Cries of 'no racism here' are heard from China to Chile, from Chad to the Czech Republic. In almost every country anti-racism is employed in the service of the nation. However, as we shall now see, such national claims are increasingly being tested, or placed in the context of international forms of governance that seem to disassociate anti-racism from national allegiances.

INTERNATIONAL ANTI-RACISM: CONTEXT AND CASES

In this section I shall offer a context for, and provide some brief introductory details on, the attempts made by international institutions to eradicate racism. The establishment of internationally accepted obligations in this area after the Second World War is often accounted for by reference to the feelings of revulsion aroused by Nazi racism and genocide. While not wishing to diminish the importance of this influence, other factors and other contexts also need to be considered. In *The Silent War* Frank Füredi (1998) has argued that the development of an international anti-racist consensus did not arise from purely altruistic motives. More specifically, he calls attention to the way the charge of racism was employed by the Western powers in the first half of the twentieth century in order to subvert and pathologise anti-colonial struggles. 'Race hatred', Füredi suggests, was identified both as a problem of rebellious non-Europeans and as a destabilising factor in international relations that needed to be tackled if order and stability were to be sustained. 'In the case of the colonies', noted one contributor to *The Spectator* in 1931 cited by Füredi (1998, p. 121), 'where the colour problem is most critical, the feeling of subordination, coupled with colour prejudice,

naturally develops into conscious racial hatred.' The group seen as
most liable to this form of 'racial hatred' were 'Europeanised
natives', the unpredictable, uprooted 'Marginal Man' (Stonequist,
1961). Füredi goes on to suggest that it was Western leaders' fear
of 'racial revenge' by their colonial subjects that first provoked
them into questioning the role of race in international affairs. In
other words, the West started to turn its back on race, and
became amenable to a new international anti-racist consensus,
only after it began to see 'race' being used as a focus of solidarity
against its own interests.

Western leaders' concern to question race and challenge racism
was also bound up with another fear: that non-white people and
nations would ally themselves to anti-Western states that
supported colonial liberation. For a number of years this worry
was focused on Japan. It is pertinent to recall that some Japanese
politicians in the early and mid-twentieth century sought to
depict their country as the leader of the 'coloured' or 'non-white'
people of the world against the West. This sentiment was one of
the factors that lay behind the Japanese government's attempt to
include a clause on racial equality in the League of Nations
Charter, adopted in 1920 at Versailles. Although blocked by the
USA, Australia and Britain, Japan's diplomatic effort established
the country's ability and willingness to act as a voice for non-
white peoples (Naoko, 1989). Indeed, in 1935 W. E. B. Du Bois
(cited by Füredi, 1998, p. 44) noted that 'Japan is regarded by all
the coloured peoples as their logical leader, as the one non-white
nation which has escaped for ever the dominance and exploitation
of the white world.'

However, the fear that the West was being 'outdone' on anti-
racism was centred for much of the twentieth century on the lure
of communism. The image of the USSR as a society without race
prejudice was once widely accepted in political circles within the
West. The danger of communist success in this area was spelled
out in 1950 by H.V. Hodson, former director of the Empire
Division of the British Ministry of Information, in a speech in
which he called for the establishment of a Commonwealth
Institute of Race Relations:

if Communism succeeded in enlisting most of the discon-
tented or the non-European races on its side, so that the
frontier between democracy and its enemies was racial as well
as ideological ... then the danger would be greatly multiplied,
and the chance of our eventually coming out on top would be
much poorer. To the extent that we solve the racial problem
itself we shall of course be preventing that combination from
coming about.

(1950, p. 305)

As these examples imply, the willingness of Western nations to
inaugurate and sustain an international consensus around anti-
racism cannot be divorced from their desire to protect their own
political interests. The construction of racism as a primitive and
destabilising force directed against Western liberty remains a
recognisable trope within the anti-racist agendas of many international agencies. Even as these institutions have grown and
become more ambitious, racism has continued to be viewed
primarily in terms of its capacity to threaten the existing global
order, i.e. as a source of conflict, a disruptive factor in the smooth
running of economies and nations. This identification of racism
with socio-economic disturbance usefully draws attention to the
association of racism and violence. However, it also means that
international agencies rarely address the role of racial consciousness and dominance within other arenas, such as cultural
colonialism or economic globalisation.

Most international organisations whose remit extends to issues
of social management have aligned themselves with anti-racism.
Having provided some general comments on the political context
of such initiatives, in the remainder of this section I shall limit
myself to some largely descriptive and comparative observations
on the anti-racist policies of three agencies of different scale and
remit: the United Nations, the European Union and the
Organisation of African Unity.

The United Nations

From its inception in 1945 the United Nations asserted anti-racism as a key principle of international relations. This concern is reflected in the United Nations Charter (Article 1) as well as within the United Nations Universal Declaration of Human Rights (1949). Article 2 of the latter asserts that 'Everyone is entitled to all the rights and freedoms set forth in this Declaration, without distinction of any kind, such as race, colour.' The UN's stance enabled the United Nations Educational, Scientific and Cultural Organisation (UNESCO) to adopt, in 1949, 'a programme of disseminating scientific facts designed to remove what is commonly known as racial prejudice' (resolution of the Economic and Social Council of the United Nations cited by Montague, 1951, p. 19). Thus UNESCO commissioned and published a series of anti-racist reports in the 1950s and 1960s (for example, Montague, 1951; Rose, 1961; Shapiro, 1965). The most important of these documents was *The UNESCO Statement by Experts on Race Problems*, released in 1950 (reproduced in Montague, 1951). The UNESCO Statement asserted that

> [for] all practical social purposes 'race' is not so much a biological phenomenon as a social myth. The myth of 'race' has created an enormous amount of human and social damage. In recent years it has taken a heavy toll in human lives and caused untold suffering.
>
> (ibid., p. 15)

Reporting the publication of this document, *Le Courrier de l'Unesco* (cited by Taguieff, 1995, p. 340) gave over its front page to announce 'Les savants du monde entier dénoncent un mythe absurde ... le racisme'. *The New York Times* (18 July 1950) proclaimed 'No Scientific Basis for Race Bias Found by World Panel of Experts'. However, the authority of the UNESCO reports was based, not merely on their claim to represent the 'most modern views of biologists, geneticists, psychologists, sociologists and anthropologists' (cited by Barkan, 1992, p. 341), but also on their ability to suggest that an international consensus had been forged, a consensus that transcended in both form and content the enmities that had led to the attempted genocides of the recent world war. This political trajectory was carried forward, albeit with varying degrees of urgency, by the UN and its related organisations throughout the late twentieth century. Building on previous work, potentially important new agreements included the UN Declaration on the Rights of Minorities, adopted in 1992, and the UN International Convention on the Elimination of All Forms of Racial Discrimination (ICERD). Although there is some overlap between the two agreements it is the latter which is the most explicit in its anti-racist objectives. It was ratified by a wide variety of member states in 1969 (it had 134 signatories by 1994). As its title implies, the Convention requires signatories to pursue policies to expunge racism. Article 2 sets out their general obligation 'to pursue by all appropriate means and without delay, a policy of eliminating racial discrimination in all forms and promoting understanding among all races'. More specific requirements include the guarantee of equal treatment within the criminal justice system and the prohibition of the dissemination of race hate literature. Signatories are required to submit reports to the UN's Committee on the Elimination of Racial Discrimination every two years (see, for example, Banton, 1994a, 1994b; also Banton, 1998). However, the fact that the Convention has few real sanctions against non-compliance means that it is essentially self-enforcing, something that has undermined its credibility in the eyes of its critics.

The European Union

The UN's desire to transcend race may be contrasted with the approach of the European Union (EU). Given that the very notion of the EU sustains a racial conceit by suggesting that the category 'Europe' provides a valid and natural basis for the establishment of a political organisation, its interest in this area is always liable to ambiguity and contradiction. The European Commission has, however, become receptive at least to the idea of the establishment of various pan-EU anti-racist initiatives. These initiatives have avoided engaging the EU's own controversial measures to harmonise immigration policy, and have concentrated on countering 'race-hate' groups and attacks. Attempts to integrate policy in the latter area, and make the incitement to racial hatred illegal across Europe, were developed by European Union interior ministers in 1995. However, it is indicative of the way anti-racism remains a jealously guarded national tradition, that these proposals were vetoed by the British Minister, who explicitly counterposed the benefits of national to international anti-racist policy: 'I believe our laws should reflect conditions in our country', the Minister noted (Howard, cited by Wintour, 1995; also Bates, 1995). 'Circumstances in other countries differ.'

The difficulty of producing pan-European anti-racist policy has meant that efforts in this area have tended to be concentrated in statements, declarations and acts of cultural symbolism. Thus the effectiveness of the EU's Consultative Commission on Racism and Xenophobia (founded in 1994) as well as the European Parliament's 'Joint Declaration Against Racism and Xenophobia' (1990), 'Resolution on the Resurgence of Racism and Xenophobia in Europe and the Danger of Right-Wing Extremist Violence' (1993) and other similar statements has yet to be seen. The same can also be said of the European Monitoring Centre for Racism and Xenophobia (founded in 1997), an initiative derived from the work of the European Parliament's Committee on Civil Liberties and Internal Affairs. According to Cross (1997) the Centre will aim to 'take stock of and evaluate racist and xeno-phobic phenomena and analyse their causes' and 'formulate concrete, practical proposals to combat these phenomena'. However, what this means in practice remains, at the time of writing, unclear. Indeed, for many, the ponderously bureaucratic nature of the EU's activities in this field (see Leman, 1996), as well as the announcement that 1997 was the European Year Against Racism, to be marked by various cultural events across Europe, have only compounded the sense that the EU has yet to resolve the nature of its commitment to anti-racism.

In part the often symbolic nature of anti-racist activity within the EU may be explained by reference to the fact that a wider pan-European body, the Council of Europe, is seen as providing protection in this area. Indeed, many commentators assert that the most effective anti-discrimination measure within Europe has emanated, not from the EU, but from the Council's European Convention on Human Rights. By 1997 36 of the Council's 40 members had signed the Convention. First signed in 1950 (by 14 states) Article 14 asserts that Rights and Freedoms mentioned in the Convention should be 'secured without discrimination on any ground', including 'race, colour'. However, no general non-discrimination clause is included in the Convention, nor are the complaints procedures (which, from 1997, proceeded through the European Court) for those who feel they have been racially discriminated against at all accessible. Indeed, despite its renown, the Convention, in the words of one leading authority, MacEwen (1995; see also Rotaeche, 1998), 'has had little impact on reducing racial discrimination' (1995, p. 62).

The Organisation of African Unity

The tensions involved in a racially defined organisation attempting to establish an anti-racist agenda are less apparent within the Organisation of African Unity (OAU), which seeks to provide a co-ordinating administration for the whole of the African continent (inclusive of Arab, Black and, indeed, European heritage traditions). The OAU, founded in 1963 by 32 African states, describes itself as 'the symbol and embodiment of age-old panafrican yearnings' (OAU, 1998). It sought to co-ordinate the decolonisation process throughout the continent, including encouraging resistance to the apartheid regime within South Africa and promoting cultural solidarity within the African continent. Increasingly, however, the resolution of conflicts within and between the OAU's member states, often defined as racial or ethnic conflicts, has become central to its activities. The task of 'transcending ethnic and national boundaries' (Salim, 1996, p. 232) is claimed to be a vital component of the OAU's attempt to establish a viable African Economic Community based on the model of – and, in part, made necessary by – the European Economic Community. However, a fundamental problem with the OAU's mission in this area is that the Organisation declared at its foundation that the national boundaries established during the colonial period were inviolable.

The OAU co-ordinates military and political exercises in 'ethnic conflict resolution' that can return states to peaceful co-existence. The African Charter of Human and People's Rights, adopted by OAU members in 1981, provides specific protection in Article 2 against discrimination by 'race, ethnic group' and 'color'. The implementation of these protections is monitored by the African Commission on Human and People's Rights, which considers, among other things, reports filed by individual member states. The March 1991 proceedings of the Commission (Human Rights Library, 1998), which considered a report on Rwanda, may be taken as an example of its attempts to challenge what it defines as 'racial' and 'ethnic' conflicts between African communities. In their summary of the evidence the Commissioners found that the Rwandan government's use of 'ethnic quotas' in favour of the Hutu majority amounted to 'racial discrimination', and violated both Article 2 of the Charter and the International Convention on the Elimination of All Forms of Racial Discrimination. The Commissioners' judgement may also be taken as illustrative of the desire to deploy the rhetoric of anti-racism within contexts often perceived previously entirely through the language of ethnicity. It seems that the charge of racism carries an impact, legally, socially and historically, that encourages its employment in contexts where accusations of 'ethnic discrimination' or 'cultural animosity' appear both inadequate and misleading.

MARKET ANTI-RACISM?

The reliance of capitalism on racism has been documented and analysed many times (Cox, 1970; Castles and Kosack, 1972; see also Miles, 1982, 1989). However, although historically proven, this link does not establish either that other economic systems have not or cannot sustain racism or that the association between capital and anti-racism is entirely antithetical. The latter relationship has attracted a growing body of commentary over recent years (Bonnett, 1993a; Cruz, 1996; Füredi, 1998). One of the most productive arguments that has emerged from this work is that while the free market has produced, or created spaces for, anti-racism, it is anti-racism of a particular kind. As one might expect, 'market-sanctioned' anti-racism tends to be oriented towards incorporating and conceptualising racial equality within its atomising, individualising social dynamic. It also exhibits a tendency to be focused on the task of breaking down those particular barriers of prejudice that inhibit the mobility of labour and money.

Discussion of the relationship between anti-racism and capitalism has traditionally been dominated by the issue of abolitionism. Western racial slavery has been viewed as rooted in mercantilism by some observers, while to others it is an early and paradigmatic illustration of the workings of capitalism. However, whatever its role in the founding of Western slavery, it is clear that capitalism was intimately involved in its ending. Abolition in Britain occurred after slavery's economic rationale had become questionable. Increasingly, it was viewed as irrational, economically, intellectually and morally. The opposition of the eighteenth-century *laissez-faire* economist Adam Smith to slavery drew these three strands together into a vision of capitalism as a force of universal emancipation, and of free market societies as places where prejudices would wither and hierarchies would be based purely on merit. Indeed, as Turley (1991, p. 232) has explained, 'the overwhelming majority of [English middle-class] abolitionists ultimately became free traders'. This set of associations has provoked many critics to suggest that the abolitionist movement was part of a process of capitalist renewal (Williams, 1966, 1970). James curtly reprimands more sentimental interpretations of abolitionist endeavour:

> Those who see in abolition the gradually awakening conscience of mankind should spend a few minutes asking themselves why it is man's conscience, which had slept peacefully for so many centuries, should awake just at the time that men began to see the unprofitableness of slavery as a method of production in the West Indian colonies.
>
> (cited by Fryer, 1984, p. 207)

As an amoral social force and one, moreover, that benefits from the subversion of working-class solidarity, capitalism may seem a strange partner of anti-racism. And yet, many proponents of market economics posit racism as an enemy of a socially and geographically mobile, and therefore flexible, work-force and explicitly or implicitly advocate anti-racism as part and parcel of capitalist regeneration (Gabriel, 1994). Furthermore, the past few decades have seen numerous examples of capitalist businesses developing race equity policies. As this implies, anti-racism is not necessarily threatening to market relations. It may, indeed, be judged to be of utility to their survival and growth. Nevertheless, the nature and implications of this relationship depend, in part, on the form and context of capitalist relations. More specifically, the role of anti-racism within state interventionist, or welfare, capitalism may be usefully contrasted with its role within neo-liberal capitalism. In the remainder of this section I will first of all draw out this comparison before exploring the formation of so-called 'corporate equity cultures'.

Anti-racism, welfare capitalism and neo-liberalism

Within Western societies, anti-racist policy initiatives are often associated with government and the public sector. It would be a mistake, however, to imagine that this connection means that such initiatives are not shaped by the needs and nature of the capitalist economy. As this suggests, rather than positing state initiatives and capital as two discrete forces it is more useful and accurate to identify their mutual dependency. As understood by its principal theorist, Claus Offe (1984, 1985), welfare or late capitalism represents a more advanced and complex form of capitalism than *laissez-faireism*. He notes that the increasing commodification of the social and natural world, and the related expansion of the ideologies and practices of consumerism, are dependent upon the development of an educated, socio-economically mobile and ideologically enculturated population. In order to create such an educated, self-motivated society a welfare sector is required capable of providing educational, health and other social interventions beyond the means and organisational capacity of the business community. This welfare sector is integral to capitalism but structurally at a remove from the ethics and praxis of the free market. It is, Offe (1984, p. 48) explains, 'foreign to capital', yet capital is dependent upon it. 'The embarrassing secret of the welfare state', Offe (ibid., p. 153) continues, 'is that while ... capitalism cannot exist with, neither can it exist without, the welfare state.' The ethos and ideologies of the public sector reflect its contradictory location within welfare capitalism (see London Edinburgh Weekend Return Group, 1980; Bonnett, 1993a). On the one hand, it is egalitarian, asserting that people's needs should be met regardless of their race, gender or ability to pay. On the other, it is concerned to facilitate the successful development of the capitalist economy. Thus, for example, in education, students are granted 'equality of opportunity' but also appraised, separated into winners and losers and socialised to participate in an anti-egalitarian market society. As this implies, welfare capitalism creates contradictory political spaces; spaces of both resistance and capitalist reproduction, spaces that are both integral to, but removed from, the survival of free market mechanisms.

It is within this contradictory political dynamic that the development of anti-racist social provision in welfare capitalism must be placed. The public sector's response to, and interpretation of, the claims of unfair and discriminatory treatment made by racialised minorities have, of course, varied considerably between different advanced capitalist societies. However, although diverging in scale, chronology and ideological heritage, these responses share three attributes. First, the establishment of an association between the public sector and equity initiatives. Second, the privileging of equity stratagems that address inequality while not directly undermining or questioning the individualistic and competitive dynamics of capitalist society. This latter focus helps explain the remorseless assertion of the rhetoric of 'equality of opportunity' and 'cultural harmony', as well as of the individualistic concepts of 'self-image' and 'self-respect' enhancement. Thus equity initiatives tend to be characterised by the ambition to create a 'level playing field', rather than a challenge to the existing socio-economic order. However, it is important to note that the former ambition may not be possible without at least raising the spectre of the latter. This brings us to the third attribute of public sector equity work. For the creation of people and institutions dedicated to equality of opportunity is not an entirely predictable process. The insertion of equity initiatives within a society where inequality is a core and structuring dynamic produces the potential for forms of action that are anti-capitalist and confrontational in nature. The institutionalisation of anti-racist radicalism in a handful of Local Education Authorities in England in the early 1980s is an example of this tendency (for discussion, see Troyna and Williams, 1986; Bonnett, 1993a). Although subsequently crushed by more dominant political forces, it is important to remember that these radical initiatives were sites of resistance produced within and against capitalism.

At a more general level, capitalism can be seen to be, in various and often contradictory ways, complicit with the formation of anti-racist consciousness. The egalitarian dynamics of universalism and relativism are often threaded through capitalist endeavour, although the role and strength of each discourse are historically and geographically contingent. The notion of a universal 'rational economic Man' (*sic*), the archetypal figure of capitalist logic, is clearly of interest in this respect. This archetype considers the world instrumentally, his actions always tending towards the maximisation of profit for the minimum of effort. Such economic efficiency, or so the theory goes, is hindered by racial and ethnic prejudice (Sowell, 1981, 1990). Wallerstein (1991) locates 'universalism versus racism' as one of the central and persistent 'ideological tensions of capitalism'. Capitalism, he accepts, 'begets racism', yet

> Anything that uses as criteria for evaluating goods, capital or labour-power something other than their market value and then gives these other valuations priority makes the item to that extent non-marketable ... It would follow that within a capitalist system it is imperative to assert and carry out a universalist ideology as an essential element in the endless pursuit of the accumulation of capital.
>
> (ibid., p. 31)

The debate about these contradictory dynamics has, as yet, remained a relatively parochial one, being largely confined to Western nations. However, another arena of contradiction and potential may now be seen interacting, overlapping and, at least in part, superseding, the processes identified above. The neo-liberal 'new world order' is often caricatured as simply a process of economic liberalisation, a synonym for privatisation and the 'taking over' of formerly protected national economies by foreign business interests. If understood in this way neo-liberalism becomes the antithesis of welfarism, the two being construed as discrete paradigms of capitalist development. However, this interpretation is misleadingly simplistic. For within both Western and, perhaps especially, non-Western societies, neo-liberalism is also about new forms of social engineering, of governmental and quasi-governmental management and social and economic intervention. It is pertinent to recall that the establishment of complex and efficient modern capitalist societies, as the theorists of welfare capitalism have shown, is dependent upon the development of co-ordinating, enculturating and educational activities that can physically and ideologically create and sustain a population capable and willing to engage in a highly mobile and complex economy. This does not mean, of course, that neo-liberalism has a discrete or identifiable 'welfare component'.

Readers will hardly need reminding that neo-liberalism's encounters with pre-existing welfare structures have usually seen the latter scaled down or demolished. However, at the same time as such 'cutbacks' and 'rationalisations' are implemented, neo-liberalism typically enables and requires initiatives in those spheres – most typically in education, training and culture – that can facilitate the creation of an efficient and harmonious consumer capitalist society.

Two interesting paradoxes emerge from these tendencies. The first is widely acknowledged as one of the ironies of the neo-liberal paradigm, namely that it appears to require a simultaneous withdrawal and extension of the state. While the state divests itself of both ownership of sectors of the economy and direct control over certain conduits of capital, it extends its interest in the sustainability and protection of private capital as well as within those arenas of social and cultural policy seen to be capable of enabling consumer consciousness. A second paradox of neo-liberalism concerns the fact that while it has acted, for the most part, to curtail the development of equity work in the West, its effects in the 'South' have been far more ambiguous. Thus, for example, while Thatcherism and Reaganomics closed down education for equality programmes in Britain and North America, neo-liberal economic restructuring is encouraging the opening up of such initiatives in many societies in South America.

The neo-liberal 'freeing-up' of global and national economies is often associated with a move towards post-modern capitalism, a form characterised by workforce, geographical and production flexibility and the assertion of social and cultural pluralism. Indeed, writing about South America, Hopenhayn (1993, p. 99) has argued that 'Deregulation is the correlative in the practical sphere of the theoretical celebration of diversity.' This correlation posits the ideal political and cultural manifestation of neo-liberal capitalism as multiculturalism, multiracialism and 'identity politics'. It suggests that, while the globalisation of capital disseminates the ideology of capitalism, it also enables, or even necessitates, a greater openness on the part of business to ethnic and racial difference.

This complex process is hard to illustrate concisely but, no matter how hard I try, whenever I think about it I am reminded of a self-consciously multiracial television advertisement for Coca-Cola, screened in many different countries from 1971. In this advertisement the camera swooped over a field of young, good-looking representatives of various 'racial types'. Each clasps a bottle of the product. Upon each bottle the familiar red logo of Coca-Cola, momentarily caught by the camera, is seen in Arabic, Chinese and other languages. The assembled mass, led by a young blonde white woman, sing 'I'd like to teach the world to sing in perfect harmony. I'd like to build the world a home and furnish it with love.' Here the commodity – Coca-Cola – coheres and gives meaning to the human variety on display. The message is multiracial, multicultural but also universalist; people can live 'in perfect harmony', when brought together within white, American commodity culture.

As this example implies, the association of neo-liberalism with multicultural *relativism* acts to obscure the fact that ideologies of anti-racism and multiracialism are being promoted within liberalising economies as both celebrations of difference and (re)affirmations of universal values and rights. Some instances from the promotion of anti-racism within Peru in the late 1990s may help to further clarify this point. Peru's economy has experienced intensive liberalisation since 1990. The process of 'freeing up' the economy has been widely understood to be bound up with 'freeing up' Peruvian society. In other words, of overcoming barriers of prejudice and bias, especially those of ethnocentrism and racism, that inhibit the geographical and social mobility of the population. The President associated with 'freeing up' and 'opening up' Peru, both to new ideas about equity and the restructuring effects of neo-liberalism, Fujimori, explains that his 'goal is to end all privileges and install efficiency and healthy competition. In sum we want opportunities for everyone' (Fuijimori, 1995, p. 441). Both these neo-liberal projects, economic and social, are conceptualised under the notion of 'democratisation'. Noting that most anti-racist work in the country is supported by USAID, the aid agency of the government of the USA, one critic explains that anti-racism and multiculturalism in Peru reflects

> a lot of influence of global interests, this idea that we need to learn how democracy is, we need to be a more civilised country, we need to learn how to live together ... From the official point of view you don't need internal conflict in a country [for it] to develop. A developed country is a better member of the international community, inter-ethnic conflict is not good business.
>
> (Oliart, cited by Laurie and Bonnett, forthcoming)

As this implies, the contemporary anti-racist movement in Peru cannot be construed as simply the product of a national or organic struggle. It has emerged from the interaction of local resistance to racism and the forces of neo-liberalism. It is interesting to note, in addition, that the concept of anti-racism (as well as overlapping terms such as multiculturalism and interculturalism) appears to many activists in Peru as an import, to be arriving in their country from North America or Europe. Whether resented or welcomed, 'Western anti-racism' is increasingly unavoidable. Indeed, the organiser of one annual 'anti-racist' festival in Lima (again, sponsored by USAID) explained to me that, in order to please the event's sponsors, he had to describe the event as 'anti-racist' rather than use the distinctively Peruvian concept of class and ethnic discrimination known as *cholism*: 'I wanted to use the idea of *cholism* in the festival,' he complained, 'I didn't want to use "anti-racism", but it is more acceptable' (cited by Laurie and Bonnett, forthcoming).

The 'corporate equity agenda'

A distinctive, if far from unique, feature of corporate anti-racism is its characteristically reactive nature. By their very nature, capitalist businesses are unlikely to place the forging of an anti-racist society as their primary goal. However, if it seems to facilitate the creation of profit, many are content to align themselves with anti-racist currents. This reactive mode explains, in part, why the corporate sector is often overlooked in debates upon anti-racism. Indeed, within countries where the state has traditionally been seen to have the main responsibility for forging social cohesion, the private sector has tended to have little interest in such matters. However, within countries where greater emphasis is placed on the social role of capitalists, the development of anti-racist policies among larger firms has, in the past thirty years or so, become common place. This is particularly so among companies conscious of their public profiles, and responsive to community or government pressure. North America provides the clearest examples of each of these factors. The 'corporate equity agenda' apparent in the USA includes measures associated with, and sometimes prescribed by, government, most notably contract compliance and affirmative action. However, it has also enabled more organic, business-led, equity ideas and practices. A prime example is 'diversity management'.

Diversity management is premised on the notion that only by drawing on the talents and perspectives of a broad range of the populace, rather than merely middle-class white males, can businesses understand, hope to sell to, and be sustainable within, the entire community. It contains a, sometimes implicit but very often explicit, critique of racism within traditional management bureaucracies. A prominent right-wing critic of diversity management, Dinesh D'Souza (1995, p. 327), estimated in 1995 that 75 per cent of the workforce in the USA are subject to 'diversity-related initiatives'. D'Souza appears somewhat mystified as to why the private sector should indulge such tendencies. Compliance with community and government pressure is one reason. Yet it does not quite explain the enthusiasm with which many large corporations have embraced this project. John Edwards (1995), drawing on equity practice within an unnamed 'large chemical organisation', has accounted for the formation of an 'equity agenda' among corporations in the USA by reference to the development of what he calls an 'equity culture', with its own rationale and goals.

That affirmative action has taken on a momentum of its own, separate from the demands of compliance, diversity, insurance and demographics, is illustrated by the response of the ... company when it found that its performance [in recruitment, employment and promotion equity] was below that of a number of other chemical companies. [The company] meets annually with twenty other chemical companies to compare progress on affirmative action. In 1980, as a result of these meetings, [the company] discovered that its progress was below average ... This acted as a strong motivator; there was 'pride at stake' and just as if the competition had been over profits, [the company] wanted to be at the top. The Affirmative Action Committee (at senior management level) therefore decided on an annual target of a 45–50 per cent minority and female intake into management streams for college graduates until [the company] was at the top of the affirmative action performance list.

(1995, pp. 148–149)

As with some of the other spheres where anti-racism has been developed, corporate 'equity culture' is unstable and changeable. D'Souza's (1995, p. 335) attack on what he calls 'an ideological movement masquerading as a booster of corporate profits' implies that it is a phenomenon dependent upon political fashion and the work of a relatively small group of equity activists who have inveigled themselves into corporate consultancy. This portrait suggests that 'diversity management' has only shallow roots in the business sector. Yet, although the short history of this phenomenon makes generalisation necessarily speculative, the evidence from the USA does suggest that alliances of business and anti-racism are possible. It also suggests that in order to be sustainable this relationship requires a variety of facilitating factors, including government pressure, a level of public sympathy and the development of a 'corporate equity culture'.

CONCLUSION

In certain circumstances, in certain countries, racial equity has been construed as radical, as subversive. Yet this relationship does not exhaust the roles anti-racism may take in relation to nation-building, international government or to capitalism. The position of anti-racism in relation to these forces is not a fixed or, indeed, stable thing. Capitalism enables racism, as many studies have detailed. But it may also enable its opposite. Similarly, racism and nationalism are often indistinguishable, yet anti-racism is often deployed by states and other national agencies in order to promote and otherwise cohere the nation. The question then becomes, what kind of anti-racism do these forms of relationship enable, what kind of anti-racism is congruent with the interests of nationalism, international government and capital? As we have seen, the answer to these questions is necessarily contingent on the particular political context within which these relationships are enacted. However, it is clear that the predominant tendency is to deploy anti-racism as a force of social stability. In other words, anti-racism is introduced as a means of dissipating conflicts understood to threaten the nation, the international order or the accumulation of capital.

3

PRACTISING ANTI-RACISM

INTRODUCTION

To be 'anti' something implies a degree of effort. To describe oneself as 'anti-racist' suggests one is prepared to act against racism, to do something about it. The question that such a self-identification invariably elicits is a practical one, 'how?'. How do anti-racists oppose racism? How do they turn their opposition into action? These questions need to be asked not merely of the small coteries of activists who position themselves within 'anti-racist movements' but also of the much broader constituency of people and policies that oppose racial inequality. As this suggests, rather than construing anti-racism as the territory of a few specialists, it may also be understood as an area of social participation engaged in and developed by many millions of individuals around the world. This chapter, which is largely descriptive in intent, addresses both specialist and popular forms of anti-racist practice, both anti-racism conceived of as something professionals 'apply', often over a discrete period of time and within a formal setting, and anti-racism as something akin to a 'way of life', a culture of behaviour.

The instances outlined in this chapter are designed to help readers think about the ways anti-racism is practised. The cases presented are *not* provided either as illustrations of 'best practice' or as representative of the most common ways of 'doing anti-racism'. These provisos may disappoint readers looking for precisely these two things. However, the range and diversity of anti-racist practice would make such a claim misleading. As we have already seen in this book, anti-racist traditions sprawl their way through history and across geography: their practice cannot be summed up by reference to a few neat examples. Thus all I would claim is that the instances addressed here serve to exemplify certain themes that are indicative of the particular forms of practice addressed. The demarcation of these forms follows, in the main, established conventions within contemporary English-language anti-racist debate. Of course, the danger of any such division is that it suggests the existence of pure and discrete traditions. The reality is – as ever – much more complex. All of the following kinds of anti-racist practice intersect and overlap. Moreover, they are often applied simultaneously. I have delineated six forms of anti-racist practice:

1 Everyday anti-racism, i.e. opposition to racial equality that forms part of everyday popular culture.
2 Multicultural anti-racism, i.e. the affirmation of multicultural diversity as a way of engaging racism.
3 Psychological anti-racism, i.e. the identification and challenging of racism within structures of individual and collective consciousness.
4 Radical anti-racism, i.e. the identification and challenging of structures of socio-economic power and privilege that foster and reproduce racism.
5 Anti-Nazi and anti-fascist anti-racism.
6 The representative organisation, i.e. the policy and practice of seeking to create organisations representative of the 'wider

community' and, therefore, actively favouring the entry and promotion of previously excluded races.

EVERYDAY ANTI-RACISM

Much of the history of anti-racism consists of the actions of ordinary people, outside of the control of state or international agencies and often unaligned to any political party. Most antiracist organisation has arisen not from formal political initiatives or bureaucracies but from the necessity and desire of people to do something about the existence of racial oppression in their lives. I shall introduce this wide-ranging topic through a series of examples, both historical and contemporary. The first concerns the resistance to slavery and racism by peoples of African descent in Brazil.

To record only government measures taken against racism in Brazil, for example, the abolition of slavery in 1888 and the making of racial discrimination into a criminal offence (under the Afonso Arinos Law of 1951), would be deeply misleading. It would provide a history in which the ruling elite appear to have bestowed equality on the masses. In fact, the history of popular revolt against racism in Brazil does much to explain the development of official policy in the area. More than this, it has structured and shaped the nature of Brazilian society. In colonial Brazil Africans formed exclusive societies to preserve their culture and distinctive identity (for example, in Bahia the Confraternização Nosso Senhor de Baixa dos Sapateiros was open only to Anhoan slaves). It is, in part, due to the work of such groups that certain African cultural and religious practices have been maintained in modern Brazil. More active forces of resistance by African Brazilian slaves included work go-slows and, more dramatically, escape to form self-sufficient communities, called *quilombos*. Many *quilombos* were established and, despite fierce assault, sustained from the seventeenth century. As Vieira (1995a, p. 30) notes, they 'had to be well organised to maintain their freedom and, whilst they existed, represented the enduring hope for a free society'. Other significant Afro-Brazilian revolts included the Sastre Rebellion of 1798, which aimed to establish a non-racial republic and, on a smaller scale, the 1807 rebellion of Muslim Hausa slaves. The leaders of the latter revolt sought to seize slave ships in order to enable their community's return to Africa. They also called for the murder of white people, either by poisoning them at public water fountains or in their homes. The Hausa and Sastre rebellions were both crushed, their leaders caught and hanged by the state authorities. However, such episodes of resistance form a continuous theme in Brazilian history. Indeed, when it came, the abolition of slavery in Brazil was widely perceived to be the result of popular agitation. An 1898 editorial in *Rebate* explained:

> Had the slaves not fled en masse from the plantations, rebelling against their masters ... Had 20,000 of them not fled to the famous *quilombo* of Jabaquara, they might still be slaves today ... Slavery ended because the slave didn't wish to be a slave any longer, because the slave rebelled against his master and the law that enslaved him ... The May 13th [abolition] law was no more than the legal sanctioning, so that public authority wouldn't be discredited, of an act that had already been consummated by the mass revolt of the slaves.
>
> (cited by Andrews, 1994, p. 308)

However, popular anti-racism (and its antecedents) should not be conflated simply with dramatic acts of mass revolt. The everyday songs, jokes and conversations employed by subject peoples across the world to mock and criticise their colonial and/or racial masters can also represent forms of engagement with racism. Such material is, it must be admitted, often difficult to discover or recover in any reliable form. However, thanks in large measure to the work of North American historians, we now have a number of well-documented accounts of the development of African American popular political consciousness in the nineteenth and early twentieth centuries. Two of the most important contributions to this literature are Eugene Genovese's (1976) *Roll, Jordan, Roll: The World the Slaves Made* and Lawrence Levine's

Black Culture and Black Consciousness: Afro-American Folk Thought from Slavery to Freedom (1977). Both works emphasise the intimate and quotidian nature of resistance. Levine's study is replete with jokes, songs, stories, and other forms of everyday discourse that act to mock white authority. Folk song lyrics containing clear social commentary – 'White folks he ain't Jesus, he jes' a man, grabbin' biscuit out of poor nigger's hand'; 'White man think he smart, / Niggers thinks he's dumb' (ibid., p. 254) – are cited by Levine alongside more ambiguous songs and stories that offer highly coded or unclear messages of refusal. The inclusion of the latter material appears to be crucial for the examination of everyday anti-racism. For, rather than attempting to reduce all his data to a narrative of dissent or to the embryonic form of Black Power consciousness, Levine shows that popular culture works at a variety of levels. It often contains 'anti-racism', but this is not necessarily the cause or horizon of its creativity and meaning.

> To argue that Negro secular song has functioned primarily or even largely as a medium of protest would distort black music and black culture. Blacks have not spent all their time reacting to whites and their songs are filled with comments on all aspects of life. But it would be an even greater distortion to assume that a people occupying the position that Negroes have in this society could produce a music so rich and varied with few allusions to their situation or only slight indications of their reactions to the treatment they were accorded.
>
> (ibid., p. 239)

This perspective may usefully be applied to many other forms of everyday anti-racism. For such forms are typically engaged in challenging racism at the same time as reproducing or developing other aspects of social identity. This conclusion is further supported by the fact that there are certain spheres within everyday life where anti-racism has found more fertile ground than others. Thus, although anti-racism may be discerned in almost every area of popular life, its presence has been particularly marked within cultural production (especially music), youth cultures, media and religion. The question of why anti-racist ideas and practices have developed particularly strongly in these fields may, in part, be answered by reference to their character-istic ability to communicate the expressive and socially challenging content of everyday anti-racism. Anti-racism has a message, it is a discourse of change. Thus those activities which are more amenable to political inflexion, more expressive of socio-cultural change, are more likely to be employed in its service.

The potential for political engagement evident within these areas is also shown by their responsiveness to political and social fashion. As this implies, anti-racist popular culture is sometimes characterised by its mercurial nature: the songs of resistance change; the slogans from the pulpit adapt to new circumstances. Within contemporary Western societies this process has become interwoven with the commercialisation of popular culture: glam-orised images of resistance being hyped and sold to each new generation of cultural consumers. This has resulted in the production of highly aestheticised versions of anti-racism. Thus, we find anti-racism reformulated as style (Hebdige, 1979). To take a fairly typical British instance, the youth music and fashion magazine *i-D* (subtitle: *Fashions, Clubs, Music, People*) offered its readers a 'Special Anti-racist Issue' in 1994. It was an edition filled with anti-Nazi imagery, 'spokespeople for positive, multi-cultural pop', and 'young, gifted and black' designers, models and artists. Within Britain and much of Europe, such produc-tions are most comfortable with anti-racism constructed as a form of generational conflict (with racism being connoted as a dated value-system) and as opposition to neo-Nazism. Thus, this form of popular anti-racism is defined against a notion of 'traditional' or 'establishment' culture as well as against the attraction of, similarly aestheticised, neo-Nazi (for example, racist skinhead) youth style, music and media. Indeed, a distinctive claim, repeated throughout this issue of *i-D* and, indeed, throughout much youth-oriented, culturally focused, anti-racism, is that a 'new generation' of multiracial youth is being, or has been, created; a generation that is subverting traditional, 'mainstream', racist culture. Thus 'youth culture' is posited both as a site for cultural experimentation and as an anti-racist society in embryo (see also Jones, 1989).

MULTICULTURAL ANTI-RACISM: AFFIRMING DIVERSITY, ENABLING EMPATHY

There are few modern national leaders who do not identify the territory they govern as culturally diverse or who do not claim to be managing, and accommodating, this diversity. Considered in this light, the practice of multiculturalism appears a pervasive component of government and administration, a component designed to achieve a sustainable state and economy. However, multiculturalism may also be defined with other aims in mind, namely the eradication of racism and/or the recognition and affirmation of cultural plurality. It is these last two approaches that have dominated debate on multiculturalism, becoming identified with the dissemination of the term and its associated practice. Although this practice tends to be regarded as a recent one, it has clear connections with traditions of relativism and cosmopolitanism, as well as with anti-colonialism and the critique of Eurocentrism. Hence the intellectual heritage of multiculturalism may be traced to those who asserted that cultural dissimilarity should not be confused with cultural hierarchy.

A complicating factor in interpreting this heritage, and the praxis into which it has fed, is that multiculturalism has different political meanings within different countries. In some countries, such as in the USA in the 1980s, multiculturalism has acquired a radical, almost insurgent, meaning: it is often construed as a challenge to the status quo, more specifically the Western or white domination of knowledge (see Goldberg, 1994; also May, 1998). In other societies, however, multiculturalism has tended to be interpreted simply as the celebration of cultural diversity, and not as a necessarily subversive programme. Another approach is to conflate multiculturalism with 'bi-culturalism' or 'intercultur-alism'. The latter two stances share many of the assumptions of multiculturalism but each has tended to be used far more explicitly to cohere, and encourage cultural co-operation between a specific and limited number of groups.

The variety of approaches we see around the world all trading under the terms multiculturalism, interculturalism or bi-culturalism has, in part, been enabled by the flexibility of the word 'culture'. Thus, for example, while some multiculturalists posit culture narrowly, as pertaining purely to community 'folk' traditions (termed by critics in the UK the three S's approach, 'saris, somosas and steel bands'), others include issues of power, economics and class within or as overlapping with culture. This divergence explains why multiculturalism can be deemed a transgressive current in one society, but a liberal or conservative device in others. However, in most cases the practice of employing culture as a euphemism for 'race' or 'ethnicity' remains a central disposition, as does the assumption that the practice of valuing 'other cultures' challenges or prevents racism. In order to flesh out what multiculturalism entails in practice I shall use two examples of its application by public professionals within state education. The two examples both derive from British multicultural education and consist of a guide to introducing 'multicultural education in schools' and an instance of a 'school exchange' between a 'multicultural' and an 'all-white' primary school.

In 1981 the Continuing Education Department of the British Broadcasting Corporation (BBC) broadcast a series of ten 25-minute in-service training programmes for teachers entitled *Case Studies in Multi-Cultural Education* (detailed in the accompanying book *Multi-cultural Education*, Twitchin and Demuth, 1981). The BBC series positioned multiculturalism as a new and socially critical paradigm, one that affects not just what is learnt in school but the relationship of the school to its surrounding community. A similar set of assumptions lay behind the school exchange I shall be discussing (I will be drawing my account of this event from a detailed depiction by two educational researchers, Grugeon and Wood, 1990). The exchange occurred between two classes of 7-year-olds and their teachers. After exchanging letters the pupils spent a day at each other's schools. In both cases multi-culturalism was deployed as both a transformatory and affirmatory process. The three key elements of the multicultural practice common to both cases are as follows:

1   'Opening up' the school to the outside world.
2   Racism as cultural exclusion.
3   Exercising the empathetic imagination.

'Opening up' the school to the outside world

The notion of schooling as a separate domain, existing in isolation from the community, is rejected by both the BBC and the school exchange initiative. A model is propounded of the school as a place that reflects and engages the world outside, more particularly the different cultural communities that exist in the school's catchment area. Allied to this position is the notion that the school's formal and informal curriculum and organisation should reflect the diversity of the nation and, to a lesser extent, the world. Thus, even if it exists in what appears to be a 'mono-cultural' region, it is suggested that the school should be a cosmopolitan and informed institution, a focus of knowledge about and interest in ethnic diversity. Examples of 'opening up' the school to the wider community offered in the BBC programmes included offering Urdu and Punjabi mother-tongue classes for parents and children and providing opportunities for British Asian parents to come into the school to share craft and folkloric traditions with the children. The theme of language provision, more particularly of challenging the complete dominance of European language skills, is given particular importance. This emphasis draws on the notion that language provides the key access point into culture. It is argued the minority student can understand her or his culture, and the majority student respect that culture, if the former's own language is acknowledged: 'it is not possible to respect the culture of any community without recognising the significance of that community's own language, or, indeed, the characteristic way in which people in that community speak English' (Twitchin and Demuth, 1981, p. 132).

Within the school exchange the notion of 'opening up' new cultural horizons was structured around the assumption that the 'all-white' school (called Garfield) was monocultural. The same conflation of colour with culture appears to lie behind the designation of the other school (called Albert Road) as multicultural because it had a significant percentage of British Asian students. It is the former school that was 'opened' to diversity, the latter that offered it. Indeed, when in their account Grugeon and Wood (1990, p.138) provide a prescriptive note that 'there is considerable educational potential within the children as culture-bearers', they evidently do not feel that they need to spell out which group they are referring to. The benefit to the pupils of Albert Road appears to have been conceived of in terms of language skills, being 'welcomed' within an 'all-white' context and through making new friends. Thus while a visit to a Hindu Temple and learning songs in Bengali were offered as core components of the Garfield pupils' trip, during the return visit the latter's home village and 'white culture' were merely a backdrop for the interpersonal and educational development of the Albert Road pupils.

Racism as cultural exclusion

Multiculturalists' concern with cultural difference implies that they are particularly alert to processes of cultural exclusion and denigration. The BBC series offered its viewers a variety of ways that educational material could be designed to facilitate cultural inclusion. Drawing on the guidelines of the New York-based Council on Inter-racial Books for Children as well as the London-based Centre for World Development Education, the theme of representativeness and representation is offered as a 'quick way' of checking children's books for racism. For example, teachers are encouraged to think about the following themes in relation to their existing stock of texts:

> Do the illustrations depict minorities in subservient and passive roles or in leadership and action roles? ...
>
> Are minority persons and their setting depicted in such a way that they contrast unfavourably with the unstated norm of white middle-class suburbia? ...
>
> Books should recognise that other cultures have their own values; they should not be judged exclusively through British eyes against British norms. Wherever possible, people from other cultures should be given the opportunity to speak for themselves.
>
> (1981, pp. 41–43)

These guidelines clearly draw on a relatively broad understanding of what the term 'culture' denotes in 'multiculturalism'. They stipulate not simply that a few symbols of other lifestyles be tossed into the curriculum but that the social ambitions and histories of 'other peoples' be represented and, indeed, that 'other peoples' should be seen to be representing themselves. These guidelines may also provoke us to consider the way 'diversity' and 'representativeness' are signified. In this example the reference to whiteness and the accompanying images of black and white children make it apparent that non-whiteness is being employed in the same way it was in the school exchange, i.e. as the key signifier of cultural/racial difference.

Exercising the empathetic imagination

The multicultural educator is rarely merely interested in confronting students with otherness. Bringing examples of Indian food and dress into the classroom is offered as good practice in both of my examples of multicultural education. Yet, in neither case, is the aim to construct classroom-bound mini-museums of cultural exotica. Rather, such exercises are designed to serve the wider purpose of enabling empathy, of generating cross-cultural understanding and solidarity. As this implies, multiculturalism is characteristically concerned with more than simply learning about others. The 'multiculturated' student is not someone who can merely list the cultural attributes of others. Rather, she or he is supposed to be able to engage and be 'comfortable' with others. Hence, the emphasis within multicultural education on enabling students to 'see things from others' point of view'. In the BBC series handbook it is explained:

> We simply cannot understand other cultures, societies and historical epochs without sympathetic imagination, that is, without rising above our own values, preferences and views of the world and entering into their world with an open mind ... It is only by means of sympathetic imagination that we can cross the space that separates us from other individuals and understand why they view and respond to the world in a certain manner. Without sympathetic imagination we remain prisoners of our own limited world ... [unable to enjoy the] diverse and fascinating achievements of the human spirit.
>
> (1981, pp. 86–89)

To 'cross the space that separates' is to develop both a wider, less limited, appreciation of 'the human spirit' and the relative nature of cultural values. Such sentiments contain an interesting irony: multiculturalism affirms difference, but for universalist ends. Indeed, the rhetorics of 'world togetherness' and 'one world' are collided and conflated with those of 'cultural diversity' and 'cultural affirmation' throughout a great deal of multicultural discourse. A popular classroom technique that brings these themes together involves instructing students to research and write about the migratory histories of their own families. Within the BBC series this latter exercise is titled 'Where are we all from?'. It includes children's family histories as well as their more immediate accounts of moving:

> When I came to school I felt very lonely because I had no friends. In Liverpool people talked differently and played

different games. They had a Liverpudlian accent. Down here no-one could understand me and I was different than all the rest.

When I first came to this school there were no Chinese people here, except in higher classes. I was the only Chinese girl in my year, and I was a bit nervous. I thought it was funny seeing coloured people – Greeks. I thought in this country there were English people. I didn't know there were so many different races.

(1981, pp. 18–19)

This particular exercise culminates in all the students' migratory movements being plotted on a map of Britain and the world, a process that appears designed to show both the diversity of routes students have travelled as well as their shared experience of being involved in migration.

Another fairly common way the themes of diversity and commonality are pursued is through twinning arrangements between schools, students and communities deemed to be sufficiently 'culturally' different. Within the exchange between Albert Road and Garfield primary schools particular emphasis was placed on the development of relationships between the students. More specifically, the desire to combine respect for difference with the appreciation of sameness is seen to be fulfilled through the establishment of *friendships*. Indeed, both the teachers and educational researchers involved in this exchange used the emergence of friendships as the key indicator of its success. When individual children indicated that they had formed such a bond it was taken as evidence of the 'crossing of barriers' and the establishment of 'new identities'. Indeed, the desire to see children getting along animated the event to such an extent that when children refused to form such emotional links their behaviour was judged 'not so hopeful' (Grugeon and Wood, 1990, p. 129), as if by their actions they were refusing to participate in multiculturalism.

PSYCHOLOGICAL ANTI-RACISM: RAISING
CONSCIOUSNESS, AFFIRMING IDENTITIES

All anti-racists are concerned with people's attitudes. However, not all forms of anti-racism are equally interested in the way people internalise and give meaning to racial and racist ideas. Two traditions that are particularly associated with placing attitudes, and attitude change, at the centre of anti-racist praxis will be described in this section. These are 'racism awareness training' and the creation of 'positive racial images'. The first tradition is almost exclusively the province of specialists or professionals in race equality. It tends to be orientated towards those who are cast by themselves or others as being racist or having the power to be so. The generation of 'positive images', by contrast, has emerged from both popular and professional anti-racism (the example I shall be using, which concerns the development of positive images of Afro-Brazilians, is rooted in popular culture) and is nearly always associated with racially excluded and marginalised communities. However, the two approaches share the assumption that anti-racism may best be effected on the level of consciousness: that to change how people feel about others and themselves is tantamount to changing society. Both approaches also share an often ambivalent interpretation of the cause of racist attitudes. On the one hand, racism is cast as ignorance. The more information on the reality of race received by those who have internalised racism, it is contended, the better their chances of rejecting prejudice. However, on the other hand, both traditions often take a less benign view of human nature: racism is cast as evil, a disease of the mind and soul that needs to be exorcised. The latter tendency suggests a mytho-poetic, revelatory anti-racism, the former a mechanical, cognitive view of anti-racism.

These two tendencies are also suggestive of the historical roots on which psychological anti-racism can draw. Most obviously, we may connect this form of anti-racist practice to universalist presumptions, especially those that evoke the essential sameness of the human race and construe prejudice and discrimination as irrational barriers that can and will be overcome by science and knowledge. Psychological anti-racism also draws on relativist ideas, especially those that suggest that different racial mores and attributes require respect and understanding. Of course, universalism and relativism may be found in a tense relationship in any number of anti-racist variants. However, in psychological anti-racism we find this relationship joined, or engaged, by other approaches. More specifically, religious discourses and practices weave their way through psychological anti-racists' emphasis on racism as sin and the banishment of racism through group or individual catharsis and confession. Another discourse that often informs psychological anti-racism is what may be termed 'ethnocentric anti-Eurocentrism'. In other words, the attempt to celebrate as central and important cultures and races devalued and excluded by Eurocentricism (a prominent example is Afrocentrism). Ethnocentric anti-Eurocentrism is not simply a reworking of relativism: it attempts to challenge the hegemony of Europe in order to construct another location from which to judge the world, not merely 'another view' but a new and different centre, with all the sense of self-worth and confidence that that claim implies.

Racism Awareness Training

The relationship between psychological anti-racism and the use of psychology in therapeutic, business and other institutional settings is reflected by the former's employment of the latter's routines (for example, counselling, group work) and rhetoric (for example, 'getting in touch with feelings', 'developing self-awareness'). Within North America and Britain Racism Awareness Training (RAT) is one of the best-known examples of this approach. Racism Awareness Training emerged in the USA in the 1970s in response to the issue of racism being forced onto the American political agenda by black activists and the popularisation of practices and notions of psychological therapy. Judy Katz's *White Awareness: Handbook for Anti-racism Training* (1978) provides one of the clearest expressions of this form of anti-racism. Many critiques of Katz's book have appeared since its publication (Sivanandan, 1985; Gurnah, 1984). In his essay 'RAT and the degradation of black struggle', Ambalvaner Sivanandan argued that 'by reducing social problems to individual solutions' RAT 'passes off personal satisfaction for political liberation' (1985, p. 20). Sivanandan went on to warn those drawn to the individualistic approach's seemingly direct engagement with white attitudes that 'catharsis for guilt stricken whites' does not contribute to the 'political struggle against racism' (ibid., p. 28).

However, by the end of the century, although Katz's terminology appeared somewhat dated, her basic approach still formed an integral part of many anti-racist initiatives. Racism, in *White Awareness*, is construed as both a symptom of ignorance and as a sickness. As noted on the book's back cover:

> In efforts to deal with that pervasive disease racism, human relations practitioners have become increasingly convinced that the American form of the disease is most effectively treated as a White problem that severely damages its White victims, as well as those against whom it is directed ... [Katz's] basic program, adaptable to any employee or school setting, is a sturdy beginning that individuals and groups can make toward genuine emotional and mental health.

As this passage implies, anti-racism is offered as a form of self-healing, a cathartic cure that is also a way of dispelling irrational fears and raising the consciousness of participants. The 'opening up' of a white participant's own racism is a central component of this process. As this implies, the tendency is to assume that all white participants are, at some level, racist; that they all share in racist culture.

RAT is usually offered as part of the training provided to employees by public or private concerns. As this implies, RAT has customarily been targeted not at self-confessed racists, but rather at people who happen to belong to an organisation that requires that its employees are not racist and/or that they evidence 'racial sensitivity'. This context, at least in part, helps explain the codified, somewhat bureaucratic, nature of RAT. Its structure and organisation reflect 'office culture', with all the time constraints and rhetorical forms that that implies. Thus RAT tends to be characterised by discrete 'exercises' (of a definite, usually short, duration), accompanied by what are claimed to be 'clear objectives' and 'achievable outcomes'.

As an example of Katz's approach, I reproduce some extracts from 'Exercise 23', entitled 'Fears of Dealing with Racism'. The following instruction and notes are provided for the session leader:

Goals
1. To have participants get in touch with fears centring on dealing with racism.
2. To help them express fears directly involving racism ...

Materials needed
Paper
Pens or pencils

Instructions
1. Ask participants to list five fears that they have about dealing with their racism. When they have completed the list, ask them to write down five fears they have that are connected to racism – a stereotype, a personal experience, a myth, and so on.
2. Ask participants to share their five fears. Continue with the second list.

Note to facilitator
1. There are two parts to this exercise. The first deals with fears of confronting racism that may be operating in the group. It also looks at reasons why people may be holding in their feelings or blocking themselves from looking at their own behaviour. Typical responses are: 'I fear discovering that I'm unalterably racist'; 'I fear being misunderstood if I start to think out loud in the group'; 'I fear that perhaps I am more racist than I thought I was'; 'I

fear that I won't have the guts, or caring, to do something about it'; 'I fear realizing my ignorance'. All these fears indicate some kind of block in the group. The facilitator must help participants not only name their fears but also explore them. It may be helpful to ask the question, 'What is the worst thing that could happen to you if your fear came true?'. This activity allows participants to get in touch with the limits and boundaries of their fears ...

(1978, pp. 98–99)

Positive identities, positive images

Psychological anti-racism is concerned with how individuals and groups internalise and 'feel' racism. Within RAT the focus is upon those construed as racist. However, the same orientation is also at work within anti-racist activities designed to enable oppressed groups to 'celebrate', 'reclaim', and 'affirm' their racial identity. Such a project overlaps with multiculturalism. We may say, more specifically, that the latter's relativism provides opportunities to display the former's concerns. Thus, for example, in the multicultural text *Positive Image* by the British multiculturalist educator Robert Jeffcoate (1979), it is explained that 'Other cultures and nations have their own validity and should be described in their own terms. Wherever possible they should be allowed to speak for themselves and not be judged exclusively against British or European norms' (ibid., p. 33).

However, it would be misleading to over-emphasise the way multiculturalism has enabled the assertion of positive racial images. The latter is a vast and multivocal project and is not dependent upon multiculturalism for legitimisation and support. Indeed, it is a paradigm that ranges from the assertion of indigenous identities in settler societies, to the development of Afrocentric philosophies within the USA and Africa; from the celebration of heroes and 'people of achievement', to the affirmation of ordinary lives and ordinary histories. It should also be noted that the example I shall introduce here, the 'black movement' in Brazil, has struggled for many years to assert 'positive images' of Afro-Brazilians, for the most part unaided by an official or unofficial 'multicultural movement'.

Brazilian sociologist Antonio Guimarães (1995) has charted African Brazilians' struggles to affirm their identity, a process that, he notes, has developed as part of an international dialogue with other African heritage peoples:

> For the African Brazilian population, those who call themselves negros (Blacks), anti-racism must mean first the admission of race; that is, a perception of themselves – the racialized others – as the racialized 'we'. It means the reconstructions of the self, drawing upon African heritage – the Afro-Brazilian culture of the *candomblé*, *capoieira*, and *afoxés*, but also upon the cultural and political reservoir of the 'Black Atlantic' legacy – the Civil Rights Movement in the United States, the Caribbean cultural renaissance, and the fight against apartheid in South Africa ... It seems that only a racialized discourse can sustain a sense of pride, dignity, and self-reliance, largely destroyed by a century of invisible, universalist, enlightened racism.
>
> (ibid., p. 224)

An early example of such praxis is the black theatre group, *Teatro Experimental do Negra* (TEN, founded 1944). Formed by Abdias do Nascimento, TEN 'sought to promote black pride through the arts, to defend black consciousness and to speak against whitening' (Vieira, 1995a, p. 35; see also Vieira, 1995b). Indeed, the arena of culture appears particularly conducive for displays and assertions of 'racial pride'. Music, art and literature have become key sites for the articulation, and celebration, of Afro-Brazilian identity. Particular attention is given to the revaluation of aspects of Afro-Brazilian life that are overlooked within Brazilian national culture and often unknown even to Afro-Brazilian people themselves. By identifying and dispelling negative stereotypes and by asserting positive qualities and achievements within Afro-Brazilian life and history, these disparate efforts have all sought to create a celebratory, but also more truthful, vision of Afro-Brazilians.

As Guimarães suggests, the development of positive images of Afro-Brazilians has tended to be tied to the assertion of a racialised reading of a black past and present, a reading in which a suppressed essence of identity is identified. Dating this effort to reconstruct 'black culture' to the 1970s Cunha (1998, p. 224) notes the key categories around which this project was structured: ' "Black culture" ' she explains, ... 'would be something to be "redeemed", "valorized", and "promoted" while kept distant from efforts to "commercialize".' Although the static view of 'black culture' implied here was challenged by some activists who sought a less racialised and more fluid view of culture (Hanchard, 1994; Cunha, 1998), the effort to create 'positive images' tended to squeeze out such considerations. The events surrounding the centenary of the abolition of slavery in 1888 may be taken as an example of this tendency. In 1988 1,702 performances, shows and other activities were officially listed, many of which consisted of celebrations of Afro-Brazilian 'dance, music, clothing, diet and other consumptive or commodified rituals' (Hanchard, 1994, p. 147). In effect, the assertion of only 'positive' views of Afro-Brazilians meant that the consideration of contemporary social inequalities was pushed off the agenda. Such an outcome appears to be an inherent danger of the desire to project positive images, but it is not an inevitable one. The campaign to assert a National Day of Black Consciousness, for example, has offered a reconstructed vision of blackness alongside a more politicised and critical view of the black past. The designated day, 20 November, commemorates the occasion of the killing of Zumbi, the leader of the independent state of Palmares, in 1695. As Turner (1985, p. 80) explains, this 'date has become a symbol of awareness and Black consciousness for many who do not recognise the "national" Black Brazilian Day, 13 May'. In particular black unity groups, such as *O Movimento Negro Unificado* (MNU), have used the occasion for demonstrations and educational work in their campaigns to both call attention to the place of blacks in Brazilian society as well as 'to validate Black culture and systematically combat its commercialization, folkloricization, and distortion' (MNU, cited by Covin, 1990, p. 133).

RADICAL ANTI-RACISM

Radicalism in anti-racism takes a variety of forms. Sometimes it refers to revolutionary politics. Indeed, within the West at least, Marxists and other revolutionaries have often sought to draw anti-racism into their project; to assert that to be a real anti-racist is to be anti-capitalist. Hence, anti-racist practice in capitalist societies becomes inseparable from the subversion and destruction of the socio-economic status quo. However, more commonly, radicalism in anti-racism is conveyed as something short of, or just different from, revolutionary praxis. More specifically, radicalism is seen as the same thing as 'social critique'. Within this latter area of activity anti-racism is construed as something that 'questions', 'deconstructs' and generally 'challenges' the presence of racism within society.

The two examples of radical anti-racism presented here are very different in scope and form. However, they each provide useful evidence of what radical anti-racism can translate into in practice. The first is Fanon's account of anti-colonial, and anti-racist, violent struggle in Algeria; the second from Godfrey Brandt's depiction of radical anti-racist teaching techniques.

Radical anti-racism as revolution: Fanon and anti-colonial war

The Algerian revolution was both far more and far less than an anti-racist war. It challenged racism, more specifically French racism, but also European dominance and capitalist relations in Africa. At the same time its widely hailed success – Algeria became independent in 1962 – did not create the kind of equal, cosmopolitan or emancipated society many of its progenitors, including Fanon, would have wanted. Fanon was deeply involved in the production of critique, most explicitly of the Eurocentric nature of psychiatry (Vergès, 1996; McCulloch, 1983; Bulhan, 1985). However, it is through Fanon's accounts of popular revolution and the possibility of creating political, non-racialised, identities that I will approach his contribution to radical anti-racism.

Fanon is quite clear that racism relies on violence. He refers in *The Wretched of the Earth* (1967) to the 'violence with which the supremacy of white values is affirmed' (ibid., p. 33). It follows, he argues, that violence is a necessary part of any challenge to racism:

> The violence which has ruled over the ordering of the colonial world, which has ceaselessly drummed the rhythm for the destruction of native social forms and broken up without reserve the systems of reference of the economy, the customs of dress and external life, that same violence will be claimed and taken over by the native at the moment when, deciding to embody hostility in his own person, he surges into the forbidden quarters.
>
> (ibid., p. 31)

Fanon constantly emphasises the necessarily popular character of this revolt. He locates the most dispossessed, the most angry, as the heart of the struggle against French rule in Algeria. Indeed, at one point he claims that 'the peasants alone are revolutionary' (ibid., p. 47) because they are most 'anarchical', the least accul-turated by Europeans: 'The country people are suspicious of the townsman. The latter dresses like a European; he speaks the European's language' (ibid., p. 89). Fanon distrusted 'the native bourgeoisie'. Indeed, he associates them with the maladies of nationalist and racist consciousness and, hence, the subversion of anti-racist revolution. When the native bourgeois comes to power, he notes:

> [it] uses its class aggressiveness to corner the positions formerly kept for foreigners ... The fact is that such action will become more and more tinged by racism, until the bour-geoisie bluntly puts the problem to the government by saying 'We must have these posts' ... If the national bourgeois goes into competition with the Europeans, the artisans and

craftsmen start a fight against non-national Africans. In the
Ivory Coast, the anti-Dahoman and anti-Voltaic troubles are in
fact racial riots ... From nationalism we have passed to ultra-
nationalism, to chauvinism, and finally to racism.

(ibid., p. 125)

Thus, Fanon attempts to map out how and why revolution
against European dominance can become corrupted. In blaming
this process on the bourgeoisie – whose 'sole motto' he claims is
'Replace the foreigner' (ibid., p. 127) – Fanon implies that only
the eradication of internal class boundaries will enable truly non-
racist and egalitarian post-colonial societies to emerge

Radical anti-racism as critique: a new syllabus

Radical anti-racist critique is designed to expose the racist nature
of existing social practices. However, the focus of this critique
varies greatly, from specific critiques of particular things, such as
one textbook, to more wide-ranging critiques of the way racism is
institutionalised and structured within an organisation or society.
One of the most well-developed areas of anti-racist critique is
education; more particularly in the anti-racist critique of the
racist nature of existing educational practice and the proposal for
new forms of pedagogy, forms that facilitate students' 'critical
abilities'. Both tendencies may be exemplified by reference to
Godfrey Brandt's guidelines for the construction of a new
syllabus,

Brandt's *The Realization of Anti-racist Teaching* (1986) provided
teachers with a practical guide to enable them to create a new
kind of learning experience and a new kind of curriculum. The
key theme within Brandt's text is the development of *critical*
thinking. More specifically, the development of students' ability
to look at existing educational material as well as the society
around them with an informed attitude to the role and nature of
racism. In the chapter dealing with the construction of an anti-
racist syllabus Brandt offers the following points that 'teachers
need to ask themselves' about new curricular material.

- Does it open up the opportunity for pupils' critical engagement with the subject matter?
- Will it help to further stimulate pupils' critical powers?
- Does it provide the opportunity for pupils to explore ways of challenging bias, racism, sexism, class domination and other forms of oppression?
- Does it address itself specifically to any, all or some of the 'building blocks' of racism and other forms of oppression?
- Does it positively acknowledge the history of struggle of Black and other oppressed people against their oppression?
- Does it explicitly acknowledge and identify the perspectives of the 'authors' of materials?
- Does it leave room for change, adjustment and new questions?

(ibid., p. 140)

The questioning nature of the education Brandt has in mind demands that students are active rather than passive learners; that they read texts with an inquisitive rather than a reverential attitude.

Brandt applies the same critical sensibility to other traditions of anti-racist activity. He depicts multiculturalism and psychological anti-racism as inadequate and conservative strategies. Opposing non-radical forms of equity work as unable to confront the depth of racism within capitalist society constitutes an important element of radical anti-racist praxis. These traditions are accused of political naïveté, of being ineffectual palliatives and distractions from the struggle against racism. Although the particular target of this hostility varies between different national and regional anti-racist debates, in both North America and Britain particular ire has been expressed about the more liberal varieties of multiculturalism. Multiculturalism 'is none other than a more sophisticated form of social control', explained Mullard (1985), 'and it has the effect of containing black resistance' (cited by Green, 1982, p. 21; see also Troyna and Williams, 1986). Thus, multiculturalism is cast as an instrument of oppression, a way for the state to co-opt racialised groups and subvert their rebellion. An interesting reflection of this approach may be found within the history of the British organisation The National Association for Multicultural Education (NAME). In 1979 NAME members in London set up a working party to critique the multiculturalist text *Positive Image* by Robert Jeffcoate. The book was described as 'muddled and dangerous' (Wright, 1979, p. 1), a typical example of the multicultural fetishisation of cultural difference and inability to tackle racism. Indeed, at the time of this debate, in the late 1970s and 1980s, anti-racism was employed by many activists in Britain as a paradigm in opposition to multiculturalism, the two being considered as mutually incompatible. Thus the relaunch of NAME in 1985 as the National Anti-racist Movement in Education was intended to signal its radicalisation.

ANTI-NAZI AND ANTI-FASCIST ANTI-RACISM

Nazism is reviled across the spectrum of anti-racist debate. However, there exists a narrower current within anti-racism that organises its activism almost solely around anti-Nazism and anti-fascism. Within this group, as elsewhere, the terms 'Nazism' and 'fascism' are often used interchangeably. However, an important distinction can be drawn between Nazism and fascism. The latter's authoritarian, nationalist and anti-democratic nature has provided fertile ground for, but cannot be said to axiomatically have led to, the development of biological racism in different countries across the world. Nazism, by contrast, understood as the ideology of the German National Socialist Party, may be summarised as a variety of fascism structured around notions of racial supremacy. It tends to be Nazism, or forms of neo-Nazism, that dominate the imagery, historical sensibility and practice of this group of anti-racists.

Anti-Nazi anti-racism may be divided into three stages. First, the anti-Nazi resistance movements active before 1945. Second, post-Second World War attempts to locate and, where appropriate, bring to trial, remaining Nazis who had escaped justice.

Third, what may properly be called anti-neo-Nazism, a post-1945 movement that seeks to confront ultra-right-wing groups who adhere to elements of Nazi (and, in the USA, Ku-Klux Klan) ideology, most especially its biological racism. It is the last of these forms of anti-Nazi activity that overlaps most completely with anti-racism. The earliest examples of anti-Nazi agitation tended to oppose Nazism for a variety of reasons. For the German Communist Party (KPD) and Social Democratic Party (SDP) the Nazis' racism was just one element of their unacceptability. They also objected to what they saw as their anti-working-class politics and, at least in the analysis of the KPD, essentially bourgeois nature. Both the KPD and the SDP actively challenged Nazism, the former being particularly assertive until 1936 (by which time it had been destroyed as a mass force by the Nazis, though see Merson, 1985), while the latter, who adopted a less overtly confrontational approach, maintained an underground resistance throughout the twelve years of the Third Reich.

The KPD developed an oppositional strategy of direct confrontation, of 'street level' propaganda and of literally fighting back against Nazi aggression. This use of political violence was premised on the notion that there existed an ideological and physical 'battle for the streets'. An example of such combat is offered below in the form of a report of a speech delivered by the leader of a KPD's Unemployed Detachment in Berlin in 1932:

> Wherever the Nazis appear and make propaganda in our district, we will impede their propaganda and drive the Nazis out ... when several Communists ... meet, say, three Nazis on the street and recognise them, they must strike them down immediately.
>
> (cited by Rosenhaft, 1993, p. 144)

Rosenhaft (1993) notes that in 'accordance with this dictum' of street level confrontation:

> local [KPD] groups spent a good deal of their time standing on street corners or in playgrounds or wandering the streets and

parks watching for Nazis. Many an apparent attack was initiated by the shout, 'There's one' or accompanied by warning to
Nazis to 'just get out of here' or 'get the hell home'.

(ibid., p. 144)

Left-wing opposition was not the only source of anti-Nazi
activism during the 1930s in Germany. Protestant, Jewish and
conservative individuals and groups were also active (Nicosia and
Stokes, 1990). In the post-war period the task of identifying and
disseminating information about Nazi racism and Nazi racists
was also undertaken by a variety of activists. The best-known
exponent of this tradition is Simon Wiesenthal (1967). A concen-
tration camp survivor, Wiesenthal began gathering evidence on
Nazi war criminals for the War Crimes Section of the United
States Army in 1945. In 1947 Wiesenthal and thirty volunteers
established the Jewish Historical Documentation Centre in Linz.
The Centre, which is now based in Vienna, collects information
on Nazis in order to enable them to be brought to trial. However,
the Documentation Centre, as well as the Simon Wiesenthal
Center established in America in 1977, are also concerned with,
and assemble material on, the rise of neo-Nazi groups and sympa-
thies. Indeed, it is towards neo-Nazism (that is, the various
far-right and self-proclaimed racist groupings that have sprung
up across the world since the end of the Second World War) that
the great majority of contemporary anti-Nazi anti-racist activity
is oriented. I will introduce this current through British examples, although similar organisations may be found in many
Western countries.

In Britain 'street-level' opposition to neo-Nazism was undertaken by Jewish groups opposing the rise of British fascism in the
immediate post-war years. However, more organised and recent
examples may be found within left-wing groups such as Red
Action and Anti-Fascist Action. Both of these groups engage in
street conflicts, their magazines being full of reports of attempts
to physically confront and disrupt neo-Nazi activism. However,
these movements remain confined to the fringes of British political life. The attempt to form a broad anti-Nazi alliance, with

mass appeal, was inaugurated in the late 1970s by the Anti-Nazi League (ANL). Although instigated by the Socialist Workers Party, the ANL attempted to mobilise a politically plural campaign against neo-Nazism. Targeting the group seen as most susceptible to neo-Nazis propaganda, white youth, the ANL staged spectacular, youth-orientated festivals (Rock Against Racism being an offshoot of the ANL) and developed a 'youth-friendly' organisational style. Thus the ANL may be said to have attempted to insert an explicit anti-Nazi component into popular culture, and to make neo-Nazism an unattractive and unacceptable option for young people.

ANTI-RACISM AND THE REPRESENTATIVE ORGANISATION

The attempt to create organisations whose employment profile and wider culture reflect the 'wider community' may utilise any of the five forms of anti-racist practice outlined above. However, the notion that organisational 'representativeness' has a role to play, or is the key to, defeating racism implies its own theory of social change. Central to this theory is the idea that victims of racism need economic and institutional power in order to lift themselves out of their marginal status. Many different pathways exist within this overall philosophy. Some routes suggest that the establishment of an elite should be the aim of such programmes, i.e. that 'lifting' a few will encourage the rest. This approach has often been favoured in the USA, where affirmative action policies have frequently been organised on the theme of 'individual achievement'. Thus, in the USA, educational entry at the tertiary level and opportunities in business leadership are key sites of affirmative action. A contrasting avenue is to attempt to 'lift' the majority of the target community. Thus, for example, within the Malaysian New Economic Policy an emphasis was placed on 'individual achievement' coupled with land grants and economic opportunities developed to benefit the bulk of the indigenous Malay population. Nevertheless, both of these approaches rely on the notion that creating multiracial organisations changes the culture of these organisations and enables them to become more sustainable and efficient in a multiracial market place and the local and wider community. Equally, both rely on the incorporation of one particular group of people as an indicator of the attainment of 'representativeness'. Thus, in the Malaysian case, the policy on indigenous Malays requires not only that this group be identified and its 'success rate' monitored but that other groups (for example, Malaysians of Indian extraction) are not assimilated within the political project to obtain racial equity. In the USA, the signifiers of racial 'representativeness' are complex and changeable. However, the key marker is skin colour. Thus the presence within an organisation of people who designate themselves, or are designated by the authorities, as not white tends to be understood as connoting the presence of 'representativeness', indeed of 'race' itself.

In many countries affirmative action on the basis of race is illegal (often being deemed to break race equality legislation) but the notion that organisations should be 'more representative' is, nevertheless, maintained as a social ideal and policy goal. This situation requires that organisations pursue a range of measures that, while not explicitly favouring any one group, act to encourage applicants from marginalised races to apply for jobs and promotion. Where taken seriously, this ambition includes job vacancies being advertised widely enough to allow a range of groups to see them and 'outreach' programmes to underrepresented populations. These activities are often informed by data on the race of existing employees. Indeed, the search for 'representativeness' nearly always involves a search for racial data. The practice of amassing employees' racial or ethnic affiliations has become standard in a variety of institutions. Once such data have been collected for a few years the organisation's aim to become more representative may be assessed. Although there exists considerable scope for action within this approach, its success is highly dependent on the commitment of the organisation undertaking it. It is vulnerable, in other words, to being treated as a paper exercise. Thus, for example, in Britain, although ethnic monitoring forms are commonplace in the public sector, the information they contain is often made little use of, while community outreach programmes remain rare. This situation was brought into focus in 1999 by *The Stephen Lawrence Inquiry* (Macpherson, 1999), a government report on the metropolitan police's mishandling of a racist murder. The report linked the lack of 'representativeness' of the police to their inability to act effectively in a multiracial city. The call of the Inquiry's author, supported by central government, for 'targets' in the recruitment of 'ethnic minority' officers was a relatively novel development in England. By contrast, although partly as a result of similar concerns, recruitment targets began to be introduced into the USA in the 1960s. Many such policies have been introduced by organisations in the private sector. However, the role of federal and state government has been crucial in both encouraging and mandating this development. My example is taken from the Presidential Executive Order that followed the 1964 Civil Rights Act, a piece of legislation that can be considered one of the bench-marks of late-twentieth-century affirmative action in the USA. The Executive Order (1965, amended) is designed to ensure that companies doing business with the government enforce affirmative action polices. It is implemented by the Office of Federal Contract Compliance Programs (OFCCP). The Order stipulates that contractors or subcontractors with a contract of $50,000 or more and employing 50 or more staff must prepare a written annual affirmative action programme, and file reports with the OFCCP that indicate compliance with the federal government's definition of an affirmative action programme. Some of the key elements of the latter are detailed by Edwards (1995, pp. 111–112) as follows:

> *Availability analysis.* An analysis of the numbers and percentages of each affected group who are 'available' for work in each job title. 'Available' in this context means living within the labor draw area for each job title, being available for work and being qualified or being capable of being trained up to qualification under the relevant job title.

> *Utilisation analysis.* An estimate of the extent, if any, of the 'under-representation' of minorities in any given job category ... 'Under-representation', which in most cases will trigger an affirmative action *plan* (active polices to increase minority representation), is defined in the regulations as: 'having fewer minorities or women in a particular job group than would reasonably be expected by their availability'.

> *Establishment of goals and timetables.* In the event that under-utilisation of minorities is found in any given job category, the contractor is required to take steps to reduce and erase such under-utilisation by a variety of measures. The first step is to set goals for the proportion of each job category that should be held by minority employees. These goals ... will normally be equal to the availability percentage for the given job category.

Although quotas are often associated with practice in this area, they are far less common than many critics assume. Indeed, the federal regulations cited here specifically proscribe quotas: 'Goals may not be rigid and inflexible quotas which must be met, but must be targets reasonably attainable by means of applying every good faith effort to make all aspects of the entire affirmative action program work' (United States Code of Federal Regulations, 1989).

CONCLUSION

Anti-racist work is often propelled by a sense of urgency, a 'just do it' imperative that privileges action as the soul of 'the movement'. However, as this and previous chapters have shown, the variety of pathways in anti-racism means that it can be 'done' in a variety of, not always complementary, ways. Perhaps the most fundamental distinction that exists within this work is a political one: while some want to find solutions within the socio-economic status quo, and believe that modern societies can be reformed to create racial equality, others see anti-racism as a revolutionary activity. Most anti-racist work is firmly within the former camp. Within Western societies, multicultural, psychological, affirmative action and most anti-Nazi activity is premised on the notion that anti-racist practice is a reformist current operating within, and accepting, the overall framework of democratic, advanced capitalism. Reformist anti-racist practice attacks racism, and may critique the existence of 'endemic racism', but it suggests that the solutions for these problems lie within the socio-economic resources of the existing society. It is an approach that may be contrasted with those groups within 'everyday anti-racism', 'radical anti-racism' (and radical anti-Nazism), who construe their anti-racist practice as part of a wider emancipatory and revolutionary project. Anti-racist and revolutionary praxis are offered as necessarily inter-related because racism and the dominant social order are considered to be mutually constitutive. Not unsurprisingly, radical anti-racism is often accused of hi-jacking anti-racism for its own political ends. The counter-accusation is that reformist anti-racism is naïve, doomed to fail and preoccupied with racism as the cause of inequality in modern societies.

This political division within anti-racist practice helps explain the alliances made and the often hostile nature of debate between activists. Activists aligned to the reformist currents detailed here routinely work together. Of course, the interaction of affirmative action, psychological and multicultural forms of anti-racism also contains tensions. The most notable one concerns the issue of racial separatism and autonomy. More specifically, an argument has arisen on whether organisations should contain, or initiatives be led by, a multiracial alliance or one particular racially defined grouping. This issue also engages the broader argument, taken up in the next chapter, of whether the end point of such activity is a non-racial society or a society where races are maintained as distinct entities.

4

ANTI-RACIST DILEMMAS

INTRODUCTION

The diversity of anti-racism means that it can appear to be in retreat and advancing at one and the same time. While one tradition is being overlooked and forgotten, another is likely to be gathering momentum. Unfortunately, anti-racist debate rarely takes its own plurality into account. A prime example of this myopia is the tendency to construe anti-racism as experiencing either boom or bust. Notions that anti-racism can be adequately summarised at any one time as 'in crisis', 'winning the day', or 'coming to an end', are usually misleading. As this implies, the anti-racist dilemmas I shall be addressing here are not offered as problems that must be solved in order for anti-racism to survive. Indeed, the tensions described might better be portrayed as part of the life blood of anti-racism; they animate its debate and provoke the heterogeneity of its activism.

Each of the four flash-points explored here touches on issues that go to the roots of what anti-racism is or could be. The issue of ethnicity is tackled first. Anti-racism has traditionally sought to see the world in terms of races, but what happens when 'the world' asserts that race is irrelevant and ethnicity is what matters? The encounter between feminism and anti-racism, the second issue addressed, has provided some of the most charged moments in the recent history of both movements. My focus will be upon how the category that dominates this interchange, 'white feminism' (or 'Western feminism'), was brought into existence by what has been called 'the challenge of the black experience' (Bourne, 1983, p. 17). The third dilemma addressed, the issue of essentialism, is of a more theoretical but no less pressing nature. It is organised around the question, 'how can anti-racism oppose racialisation when it requires races as its key agents?'. The fourth and last theme explored returns us to the group, who, within Western and much non-Western anti-racism, are posited as the centre and progenitors of racism, namely whites. Drawing on recent work in the newly established field of 'white studies', the possibilities of white involvement in anti-racism are discussed.

ANTI-RACISM AND ETHNICITY

Anti-racism did not develop purely in response to biological racism. It also arose in reaction to discriminations that drew on ideas of nation, culture and religion. Indeed, as we have seen, anti-racism may be found within a wide variety of situations where these forms of identity have been naturalised and stereotyped. Yet although anti-racism has rarely concerned itself solely with opposing the ideology of scientific racism, anti-racist rhetoric often evokes this form of racism as its primordial and primary stimulus (Taguieff, 1995). Hence, there exists a disjunction, or uneasiness of interchange, between anti-racism and debate on ethnic discrimination. We may find symptoms of this process in the hesitant way the concept of racism is deployed in discussions of national and religious conflict. In Britain, for example, racism is only occasionally invoked in claims of discrimination between, for example, the English and other European nationals, or Christians and Muslims. Indeed, when, in 1998, a tribunal awarded compensation to a Danish van driver after concluding that the abuse he received from his supervisor contravened the Race Relations Act it attracted national media attention. The supervisor, the tribunal concluded, 'may well have thought their remarks were not racist because of [the Dane] being white like themselves'. However, it ruled that 'being white made no difference in so far as allegations of racism were concerned' (Wazir, 1998). In the same year a London council, responding to a campaign by a white supremacist group against the development of a local mosque, attempted to bring Muslims under the Race Relations Act (Dyer, 1998). Reflecting the depths of confusion that surround the demarcation of the groups the Act applies to, the High Court threw out this application on the grounds that 'Muslims were a religious rather than an ethnic group and therefore not covered by the Race Relations Act'. Yet the conflation of ethnicity and race contained in this last remark is itself indicative of the possibility of expanding 'race' into identities defined around national or cultural (and presumably religious) categories.

Clearly the terminology of race and racism is already being used to understand conflicts which few would imagine to be rooted primarily in biological racism. Yet contemporary anti-racist debate in Britain, as in many other countries, tends to marginalise, or side-step, national, religious and other 'ethnic' conflicts. Such issues have a hesitant, undigested, place within anti-racist discourse. Only when matters turn to skin colour does British anti-racism appear sure of itself. A comparison of the media reaction to two recent news stories supports this assessment. In February 1999 *The Stephen Lawrence Inquiry* on the racist murder of a black teenager was released (Macpherson, 1999). In the same month another story was developing, one that was to dominate the news headlines a matter of weeks later, namely the Serbian government's treatment of Kosovans of Albanian heritage. In both cases the explanations offered by the British media centred upon processes of social exclusion and stereotyping. In both cases a dominant group was accused of harbouring prejudices of both culture *and* 'blood' against a minority group. However, the murder of Stephen Lawrence, the police treatment of it and the reason why such events could occur in Britain, were understood, almost entirely, through the concept of racism. Serbian treatment of 'ethnic Albanians', by comparison, was, as the latter epithet implies, portrayed as a consequence of 'ethnic hatred'. It is true that, every so often, a phrase such as 'Serbian racism' was applied to the situation. Yet, the nature of this 'racism', its implications and origins, remained undeveloped, effectively side-lined by explanations that gravitated around 'the fact' of 'national hatred' and 'ethnic fighting' between discrete and, seemingly, obvious entities. These latter explanations offer few opportunities for assessing the naturalisation and production of identities, more specifically the way an 'ethnic group' can come to be forged as a *recognisable* collectivity. As seen in the Stephen Lawrence case, the concept of racism can be employed to unpack such issues and to challenge the naturalisation of social difference. The British media's explanations of what was going in Yugoslavia wasted this resource.

Much contemporary English-language anti-racism appears to be structured around the conviction that 'real racism' is about what whites do to non-whites. What the Serbs and Albanians, English and Scots, Christians and Muslims do to each other is something different, something of less consequence. As this implies, many of the most important tensions of modern times have a twilight existence within anti-racism. They are occasionally framed in its vocabulary, but do not appear to have an authentic claim upon its ideas, activism or solutions. Yet it is anti-racism that offers the most developed critiques of, and responses to, inter-community discrimination, homogenisation, naturalisation and stereotyping, found in the contemporary world. The rhetorics of 'anti-ethnic discrimination' and 'anti-xenophobia' are weak and cumbersome by comparison. Partly as a consequence of race being one of the twentieth century's dominant paradigms of naturalised difference, equity activism organised around the concept of ethnicity tends to have a relatively indistinct identity. This situation may also be explained by reference to the fact that, over the past fifty years, the concept of ethnicity has managed to escape the level of damning critique that has befallen 'race'. Indeed, as early as the 1930s Huxley and Haddon (in Huxley *et al.*, 1939, p. 220) suggested that 'the word race should be banished, and the descriptive and non-committal term ethnic group should be substituted'. The notion that the word 'ethnic' (and, by extension, 'ethnicity') enables one to avoid implying 'connotations of homogeneity, of purity of descent, and so forth' (ibid., p. 221) has often made it difficult to target in struggles for social equity and tolerance. Claiming an ethnic allegiance has been allowed to appear anodyne, merely a reflection of a 'cultural choice'. And yet, of course, such claims rarely rely only on culture. If they did, 'ethnic cleansing' would be an effort of re-education and acculturation rather than of forced eviction and murder.

This problem would be eased if race and racism were understood as representing processes of naturalisation. This approach would encourage activists to identify the existence and role of racism *within* ethnic (including nationalist) conflicts, thus avoiding either ignoring such disputes or simply collapsing them into questions of race. In other words, race and racism could be approached as tendencies existing within other, broader, social processes of identity formation. This perspective would also have the advantage of engaging debates on 'ethnic difference' with debates on 'racial difference', denaturalising ethnicity and enabling anti-racism to be seen and consciously deployed in a wider variety of situations. Thus the so-called 'ethnic disputes' that erupted in the former Yugoslavia during the 1990s may be identified as being, in part, animated by racism and, hence, seen as a suitable arena for those forms of anti-racist practice discussed in Chapter 3.

However, at present, ethnicity remains a problematic area within anti-racism: it is either clumsily conflated with race or, more commonly, ignored. In part, this situation has been sustained over recent years by the notion, commonly associated with radical anti-racism, that ethnicity is merely a euphemism for race which, in turn, is essentially a question of the struggle of black people against white racism. In Britain Sivanandan (1983) suggests assertions of ethnicity act to subvert political solidarity among racialised groups:

> Ethnicity was a tool to blunt the edge of black struggle, return 'black' to its constituent parts of Afro-Caribbean, Asian, African, Irish – and also allow the nascent black bourgeoisie, petit-bourgeoisie really, to move up in the system. Ethnicity de-linked black struggle – separating West Indian from Asian, the working-class black from the middle-class black.
>
> (ibid., p. 4)

This perspective ties talk of ethnicity with liberal multicultural-ism, setting it in opposition to the political focus of radical anti-racism. More specifically, ethnicity is being portrayed by Sivanandan as a way of reducing social differences to questions of cultural choice and tradition and, hence, of avoiding the issue of racism. This critique of ethnicity (and multiculturalism) implies that radical anti-racists should avoid ethnic categories and adopt explicitly racial and/or political labels. However, as the passage cited above indicates, the racial/political categories to be privi-leged over ethnicity are, at least within the UK, based on the presumption that skin colour provides the most appropriate metaphor or fact of racial/political difference. Indeed, within British anti-racism, tension between 'blacks and whites', has come to be used as a kind of shorthand formula for all racial conflict.

'Black' has long been used to incorporate and cohere a trans-racial community of resistance. The 1805 Constitution of Haiti declared all Haitians were black, no matter what their skin colour was. 'Now when I say black', asserted one of the founders of Black Power, Malcolm X (1987, p. 12), in March 1964, 'I mean non-white. Black, brown, red or yellow.' A similarly inclusive view of blackness was asserted by the Brazilian activist Oliveira e Oliveira in the early 1970s (see Cunha, 1998). More recently such usages have been developed furthest in Britain, where blackness was recoded, and widely employed, as a political term. However, the history of the attempts to use 'black' politically in Britain provides an interesting insight into how, no matter how much the term is politically inflected, a black/white model of social difference almost invariably carries within it ethnic and racial connotations and exclusions.

An example of the articulation of political blackness may be found within Clark and Subhan's (undated) guidelines on anti-racist terminology. They state:

> Black as a political term in relation to people is not a descriptive term for the colour of skin of a person. It is a common term used to describe all people who have experienced and have a common history of: imperialism, colonialism, slavery, indentureship and racism.
>
> (ibid., p. 33)

Clark and Subhan also propose a parallel definition of 'white'. This word, they note, should be used as: 'a political term in relation to people ... Both in global terms and in the British context ... white as a political term is a term for the oppressor' (ibid.). Taken together, these definitions provide a coherent view of social classification. However, Clark and Subhan are not able to maintain this consistency. Their usage repeatedly implies the dominance of phenotype over political history. Those who have experienced Western imperialism and its attendant oppressions include a huge variety of groups, including the Irish, Native Americans and Arabs. Yet despite their own definition Clark and Subhan do not regard such people as black. 'Black people', they note, 'may be African, Caribbean, Chinese or South Asian in origin.' Although, somewhat unusually, Clark and Subhan admit the Chinese to the fold of blackness, it is apparent that, as soon as their discussion turns from abstract categorisation to a concrete list, they are proposing a racially exclusive vision of being politically black.

Another insight into the problems with maintaining a purely political and de-ethnicised form of anti-racist categorisation may be found within the anti-racist policy documents produced by the Inner London Education Authority (ILEA) in 1983. The word 'black', the ILEA first reminded its readers, is useful because it 'emphasises the common experience which both Afro-Caribbean and Asian people have of being victims of racism' (1983, p. 19). However:

> Other groups who, together with the black communities, are usually referred to as 'ethnic minorities' also suffer varying degrees of prejudice and discrimination. These include Chinese, Greek Cypriots, Turkish Cypriots, Turks, Vietnamese, Moroccans. In a similar way, though not always to the same extent, some white ethnic groups, such as the Irish and the Jews, experience prejudice and discrimination. In using the term 'black' ... it is not the Authority's intention to exclude any minority group.
>
> (ibid.)

Despite the 'Authority's intention', not to 'exclude any minority group', the ILEA's original definition of black, as referring to 'Afro-Caribbean and Asian people', clearly does exclude those it refers to as 'ethnic minorities'. However, the ILEA's phraseology is curiously ambivalent. Groups such as the Chinese and Greek Cypriots are introduced as being *usually* 'referred to as "ethnic minorities"'. It is then implied that they *may* be black. In this way the ILEA avoids responsibility for naming these people. The consequence of this manoeuvre is that these communities are positioned as marginal, both within British society and within anti-racist analysis. This impression is strengthened by the fact that, while other minorities are mentioned only rarely and briefly, 'Afro-Caribbean and Asian communities' are addressed by the ILEA (ibid., p. 24) as 'the chief victims of racism'. As with the other definitions quoted, a political definition of black is thus combined with racially specific identifications of Afro-Britons and British Asians as the real blacks.

However, British Asians' status as real blacks, as the authentic other of white society, was also in doubt within the supposedly de-ethnicised, politicised, British radical anti-racism of the 1980s. For another characteristic of the use of 'black' that we can draw attention to indicates that, not only has it been constructed as an ambiguous racial/political category, but that this phenomenon has been acerbated by a tendency to find the essence of blackness within people descended from sub-Sahara Africa. This process reflects the fact that black first emerged as a self-definition among African Americans, that within the USA it is almost uniquely applied to African Americans and that this model, and this history of resistance, has been exported across the world (Modood, 1996). It is not surprising, therefore, that the attempt to define black as a political noun in Britain was not successful in entirely distinguishing itself from this 'American' model. Indeed, Tariq Modood (1988, 1990a, 1992, 1994) draws together numerous instances of the deletion of the British Asian experience in radical anti-racism. Thus he notes how books that have promoted a politicised view of racial formation, such as Gilroy's *'There Ain't No Black in the Union Jack'* (1987a), concern themselves almost entirely with the history and culture of Afro-Britons. Noting that the 'black/white' model of society provides non-whites with an identity entirely based on their relations to whites, as victims of white racism, Modood (1990a) argues that anti-racism must take ethnicity seriously:

> Anti-racists seem to be slow to recognise that it is ethnic communities, no less than colour and class, that lie at the heart of race and race relations today. The root of this inability lies in creating race exclusively from the point of view of the dominant whites and failing to recognise that those who white people treat as no more than the raw material of racist categorisation have indeed a mode of being of their own which defies racist categorisation.
>
> (ibid., p. 92)

Modood's assertion of the importance of ethnicity is seen particularly clearly in his suggestion that the anti-racist agendas of different ethnic groups will vary according to their particular interests. Anti-racism 'ought to begin', he writes, 'by accepting oppressed groups on their own terms (knowing full well that these will change and evolve) not by imposing a spurious identity and asking them to fight in the name of that' (ibid., p. 92). More specifically, Modood is concerned with the development of a form of anti-racism that responds to and arises from the concerns of Muslims. 'Authentic anti-racism for Muslims', he writes, 'will inevitably have religious dimensions and take a form in which it is integrated to the rest of Muslim concerns' (ibid., p. 92). For Modood, as for other Muslim anti-racists, a high priority within a reformulated anti-racism is the protection of Muslim sensibilities within Britain's existing anti-discrimination legislation.

> There is now a desperate need to have religion included in the Race Relations Act 1976 ... More than anything, this simple decent act would erase the feeling of persecution, oppression and hostility felt by the Muslim towards the authorities.
>
> (*Q-News*, cited by Modood, 1993, p. 517)

The discussion paper issued by the Muslim Parliament of Great Britain (1992), *Race Relations and Muslims in Great Britain*, provides a more radical reading of the absence of protection for Muslims within the existing legislation:

> It can only be assumed that the omission of [religious discrimination from race relations laws] was deliberate and designed to prevent Muslim communities of different origin from assuming a common identity. Muslims were deliberately side-tracked into assuming false identities, just as they had been under colonialism.

Such concerns appear to have begun to influence the way the British government attempts to classify identity. Commenting on the inclusion of a question on religious belief in the 2001 National Census, the Home Secretary (Straw, cited by Travis, 1999) noted that 'there is a need ... to expand on the kind of ethnic monitoring that is carried out ... It is clear that the basic classifications of black, white or Asian are simply out of date.'

Pina Werbner (1997) ties the assertion of a distinct British

Muslim anti-racist agenda to a developing sense among young Muslims that they are marginalised in two overlapping ways, racially and because of their religion (also Modood, 1990b). Moreover, because of the way these two forms of identity are confused in British society, Werbner points out that claiming religious rights can often be a way of protesting against racism. Within Britain, the two forms of exclusion were starkly demonstrated to many Muslims by their lack of legal redress following the publication of a purportedly anti-Muslim book, *The Satanic Verses*, by Salman Rushdie in 1988 (a blasphemy law exists in Britain, but it only protects Christianity).

> The fact that the book seemed to mock and deride Islamic culture and values made it a symbol of racism, of the humiliation Pakistanis experience daily as victims of racial abuse and discrimination ... As the affair continued, it became clear that Muslim religious feelings were not protected under the blasphemy law. British Muslims discovered that their religion could be violated and mocked without the law affording them any protection. In response, in a schismogenetic process of polarisation, they essentialised English society as hostile and unfeeling. At the same time, they reconstituted themselves as a community of suffering ... For Muslims in Britain, the Rushdie Affair is experienced as a festering open wound, an unpaid debt that demands redress and moves them to claim a separate anti-racist identity in the public sphere.
>
> (Werbner, 1997, pp. 232–248)

However, Werbner, unlike Modood, suggests that the most effective forms of anti-racism work by suppressing differences rather than asserting them. Fracturing anti-racism into myriad ethnicised anti-racisms, she argues, would pit ethnic group against ethnic group and undermine the overarching moral claims generated within campaigns based on social solidarity. 'Effective anti-racist struggles', she notes (ibid., p. 247), 'depend on the evolution of common, unitary narratives and the *suppression* of cultural differences between victims of racism.'

The calls of Modood and others for an ethnically sensitive anti-racism usefully highlight the fact that the black/white binary model of anti-racism in Britain, while claiming a 'common, unitary' narrative, in fact imposed an exclusive and racially biased framework for action and theory. However, it is difficult to imagine how the fragmentary logic behind their accounts could provide firm foundations for an integrated struggle against racism. Radical critics have often charged that the language of ethnicity is employed as euphemism for race, and that it acts to divert attention away from issues of power and towards matters of 'mere' cultural expression. Assigning identities as fundamental as religion to the status of epiphenomena is testament to the vanguardist arrogance of such attacks. However, they contain an important truth: the naturalisation of ethnic difference into race, and the power imbalances that have accompanied that process, can disappear from view within an entirely fractured, ethnicised landscape of social difference.

ANTI-RACISM AND FEMINISM

The relationship between anti-racism and other emancipatory movements has rarely been straightforward. This is partly because anti-racism contains the potential to identify and question the racism within other forms of social critique. The relationship between feminism and anti-racism provides one of the most controversial of these encounters. An influential and indicative product of this intercourse has been the category 'white feminism', an expression that encapsulates many of the key insights and problems that have emerged from this history. In this section I will account for the development and deployment of this concept.

In *Beyond the Pale* Vron Ware (1992) locates one of the sites of origin for Western feminism within the efforts of Victorian 'white feminists' to attend to the plight of non-white female victims of supposedly backward and oppressive non-European societies. The claim of female empathy and solidarity was developed, argues Ware, in conjunction with a taken-for-granted

Eurocentricism that conflated female liberation with Westernisation (see also Chaudhuri and Strobel, 1992). However, this process was interwoven with a more reflexive deployment of empathy as a way of questioning white society. The American abolitionist Lydia Maria Child made the following comparison in 1843: 'In comparison with the Caucasian race, I have often said that [the coloured race] are what woman is in comparison with man. The comparison between women and the colored race as *classes* is striking' (cited by Ware, 1992, p. 69). Child also exemplifies the problem of priorities that can arise when supporting what are understood as two separate egalitarian struggles. It was Child's view that the 'race issue' was more urgent than women's rights. Her name has also been associated with what has come to be called the 'domestic feminist' view, namely that women showed their superiority to men by demonstrating a willingness to sacrifice their own interests for the sake of others. 'The suffrage of women', Child (cited by Fredrickson, 1988, p. 92) wrote in 1867, 'can better afford to wait than that of the colored people.'

Debate about 'what is more important', the struggle against racism or the fight against sexism, has continued to mark the encounter between feminism and anti-racism. Within the late twentieth century, it became increasingly common to admit to the interconnections between different forms of oppression, a situation that both encourages generalised affirmations of 'the significance' of other forms of equity work and makes interactions between them ever more intimate and ubiquitous. Within this context the process of prioritising one struggle over the other requires forms of justification that avoid claims to greater status. The affirmation of 'experience' as the key arbiter of political identity is the most influential example of such a discourse. The appeal to experience allows one to assert that, by pursuing one form of activism rather than another, one is simply responding to one's own immediate context and personal history, a claim that appears to allow other struggles and other people's concerns equal importance. However, this process exists in uneasy relation with the potential within feminism and anti-racism for mutual critique. For both feminism and anti-racism are capable of deconstructing the nature of 'experience', of questioning it as a gendered or racialised phenomenon. Indeed, it has been precisely the taken-for-granted premises of 'white feminism' that have formed the focus of anti-racist challenges. Such criticism has produced the category and identified 'the experience' of 'white feminism'. The considerable impact of such attacks has derived from the fact that they have, for the most part, been developed by other feminists, most notably non-white feminists. This process has enabled, or compelled, 'non-white feminism' to become a recognised position defined in relation to white feminism, a position from which to offer 'the challenge of the black experience' (Bourne, 1983, p. 17; see also Carby, 1982; Amos and Parmar, 1984; hooks, 1984). At the heart of this challenge has been the identification of 'white feminism' as offering Eurocentrism in the guise of universalism. This reading allows the claims of 'white feminists' to offer a model of liberation for the world to be placed within the context of European colonial power and the fact that 'white women stand in a power relationship as oppressors of black women' (Carby, 1982, p. 214). In her article 'White woman listen: black feminism and the boundaries of sisterhood', Hazel Carby identifies the way 'white feminists' deploy such concepts as 'family' and 'tradition' in a manner both ignorant and dismissive of the ways they are experienced by black women. 'Too often', she notes, 'concepts of historical progress are invoked by the left and feminists alike, to create a sliding scale of "civilised liberties"':

> When barbarous sexual practices are to be described the 'Third World' is placed on display and compared to the 'First World' which is seen as more 'enlightened' or 'progressive'. The metropolitan centres of the West define the questions to be asked of other social systems and, at the same time, provide the measure against which all 'foreign' practices are gauged.
>
> (ibid., p. 216)

Within this account 'white feminism's' universalistic presumption is set against the existence of cultural or racial differences among women. 'The feminists' slogan "sisterhood is global"', writes Avtar Brah:

> failed to acknowledge the heterogeneity of the condition of being a woman. What does it mean to be a Native American or Native Australian woman whose lands rights have been appropriated and whose cultures have been systematically denigrated by the state as well as by dominant ideologies ... What are the points of convergence and divergence in the lives of black and white women in Britain? Such questions point to major differences in the social circumstances of different groups of women, and this will mean that their interests may often be contradictory.
>
> (1996, pp. 84–85)

Brah's observations imply that there exist different types of feminist struggle. Despite the diversity of her examples, within Western feminism the assertion of non-white perspectives has often been equated with the development of 'black feminism'. More specifically, it has been associated with the latter's capacity to point to an indivisibly racialised and gendered social location and experience. One much cited defence of the irreducibility of racialised/gendered identities was offered by the Combahee River Collective, a Black feminist group founded in 1974 in the USA. *The Combahee River Collective Statement* (1986) provides a clear expression of the deployment of a 'black feminist' position, a construct that is used to both forge connections to, and provide a site of criticism for, a series of 'interconnected' oppressions:

> we are actively committed to struggling against racial, sexual, heterosexual, and class oppression, and see as our particular task the development of integrated analysis and practice based upon the fact that the major systems of oppression are interlocking. The synthesis of these oppressions creates the

conditions of our lives. As Black women we see Black feminism as the logical political movement to combat the manifold
and simultaneous oppressions that all women of color face.

(ibid., p. 9)

A different kind of assertion of the diversity of feminism is
offered by Bourne. Writing in 1983 Bourne contended that there
is virtually nowhere in 'western feminist writing ... a sense that
Third World women actually have an indigenous history and
tradition of struggle from which western feminists could learn'
(ibid., p. 19). Such interventions have provided an important
stimulus for both feminism and anti-racism. By bringing into
view the gendered and sexualised nature of racism it has become
possible to appreciate the interwoven nature of these struggles
(see also Anthias and Yuval-Davis, 1992). However, the categories of 'the black experience' and 'Third World women' that
the Combahee River Collective and Bourne use to structure their
attacks limit the possibilities of such work. This is because these
categories are defined almost entirely as oppositional entities, as
forms of resistance to 'white' or Western feminism. In this sense
they are not accorded any autonomous history or geography.

Since the early 1980s the demarcation of an oppositional
'black female constituency' has come under increasing pressure by
those who doubt its utility in assertions of 'difference'. Indeed,
echoes of the challenge to 'white feminism' as a form of colonial
knowledge may be heard in Knowles and Mercer's (1992) identification of 'black feminism' as a project dominated by the
concerns of black American and British women:

Afro-American and black British women need to recognise that
African women may not share their conception of femininity
nor their notion of oppression. This point is illustrated by the
example of a Nigerian feminist group started in 1982, 'Women
in Nigeria'. In developing a notion of black women's oppression in Nigeria, this group obviously did not attach the same
importance to racism as black British or black American
women who live in a hostile environment ... Their concerns

focused on the need for land reforms, rural development and the need to examine relations between women (co-wives) in polygamous marriages.

(ibid., p. 111)

If experience is posited as the key arbiter of political identity, then the homogenisation and erasure of experience become a key site of political dispute. 'White feminism' has been simultaneously subject to and brought into existence/visibility through this form of criticism. More recently 'black feminism' has been undergoing a similar treatment. Of course, this process could be extended even further (and it *is* noticeable that Knowles and Mercer appear to use one women's group in Nigeria to make generalisations about 'African women'). This prospect raises the spectre of the disintegration of feminism as a coherent and, hence, effective political force. It is, in part, in response to this situation that anti-racist feminists have been at the forefront of the debates discussed below on the uses and abuses of essentialism.

ANTI-RACISM AND ESSENTIALISM

Essentialism may be defined as the explanation of social phenomena by reference to fixed and/or natural essences. The last twenty years or so has seen the word increasingly employed as a term of criticism. Within the humanities and social sciences essentialism has been counterposed to a belief in the socially constructed, and, hence, historically and geographically contingent, nature of identity. This latter perspective has also come to be associated with the assertion of the value of transgressive identities, identities which cross borders and mix and subvert the established codes of racial discourse. Hence a celebration of hybridity, of hyphenated identities, syncretism and *mestizaje*, have all been connected with this tendency. 'Anti-essentialism' has emerged as an emancipatory discourse, tied to the affirmation of the mutability and multiplicity of identity.

Schor (1994, p. xvii) suggests that 'Anti-essentialism in its positive form, constructionism, has won the day.' However, as we have seen throughout this book, anti-racism has often relied on notions of fixed essence. More specifically, anti-racists have frequently posited the objective reality of race. When anti-racists have sought to 'liberate races' they have often based their activism on the existence of racial essences (for discussion, see Dominguez, 1994). Moreover, essentialism is not some marginal current within anti-racism, but weaves through almost every aspect of its historical and contemporary practice. It is anti-racists who have called for indigenous peoples' racial identity to be 'respected'. It is anti-racists who have tried to identify and cele-brate racial struggles against dominant groups. And it is anti-racists who have mobilised terms such as 'white people', 'black people', and so on, in the service of equality.

In North American academic commentary this dilemma has, in recent years, increasingly been approached through engage-ments with Charles Taylor's (1992) *Multiculturalism and 'The Politics of Recognition'*. More specifically, the significance of 'non-recognition' – particularly of the fact that cultural '[n]onrecognition or misrecognition ... can be a form of oppres-sion, imprisoning someone in a false, distorted, reduced mode of being' (Taylor, 1992, p. 4) – has been discussed in the context of claims for the importance of other forms of injustice. Comparing Taylor's focus on recognition with his neglect of economic redis-tribution Nancy Fraser (1998; see also Willett, 1998) suggests that social justice would better be served by equity in the economy and deconstruction in culture. Fraser ties these two projects together by arguing that only a socially transformatory, socialist, model of redistribution is likely to be sympathetic to a deconstructionist, anti-essentialist, approach to cultural recogni-tion. By contrast, she positions recognition politics as essentialist and as congruent with the fragmentary logic of welfare capi-talism. Fraser's critique highlights the limitations of emphasising recognition. Yet it provokes an obvious question 'what kind of equality could deconstruction serve?'. Deconstruction is, after all, famously subversive of moral or political metanarratives, socialism included.

Clearly, the rise of a debate on essentialism poses complex challenges for anti-racism. It is useful to recall, however, that these challenges are not entirely new. They were recognised long before the terms 'anti-essentialism' or 'deconstruction' were developed. Indeed, opposition to 'racial thinking' and categorisation is as old a tendency in anti-racism as racial essentialism. From Montaigne to Fanon, 'anti-racists' (and their antecedents) have strived to denaturalise, and by implication to historise and problematise, taken-for-granted assumptions about human difference. Indeed, if a novel tendency can be found within anti-essentialism it is not the questioning of 'racial essences' but in the more provocative suggestion that the notion of 'racial experiences' contains an essentialist agenda. 'Experience' is central to a lot of anti-racist discourse. Whether as experience of racism or experience of resistance, it is a theme that is seen to cement solidarities and identities. Yet anti-essentialists are necessarily sceptical of claims implying homogeneous 'racial experiences'. Theoretical work undertaken in feminism, where the notion of 'women's experience' has been placed under scrutiny, is pertinent here. For Diana Fuss:

> Even if we were to agree that experience is not merely constructed but also itself constructing, we would still have to acknowledge that there is little agreement amongst women on exactly what constitutes 'a women's experience'. Therefore, we need to be extremely wary of the temptation to make substantive claims on the basis of the so-called 'authority' of our experience.
>
> (1989, p. 25)

Grimshaw (1986, p. 85), another feminist writer, makes the observation that 'experience does not come neatly in segments, such that it is always possible to abstract what in one's experience is due to "being a woman" from that which is due to "being married", "being middle class" and so forth'. Within anti-racism the claim to 'speak for' racial experience has come under strain because of similar objections.

If only because of its relatively obscure vocabulary, it might be imagined that the tendency towards anti-essentialism is most strongly represented within academic, as opposed to popular anti-racist, debate. Activists within the latter area are, after all, obliged to engage with race in an instrumental and strategic way, employing claims of group solidarity and group identity in order to provide an effective politics of resistance. Indeed, the deconstruction of race may seem a luxury, and a self-debilitating one at that, for those who wish to mobilise around the notion of racial oppression. However, essentialism and anti-racist activism are not necessarily mutually dependent. Many activist movements have rejected the idea of race, while nearly all contain tendencies or currents that are critical of it. Thus, for example, within Afro-Latin American and African American anti-racist politics there exists a debate between those who wish to abandon and critique the notion of race and those who regard this position as either politically naïve or as a form of racial treason. Within the former camp we may place critics influenced by the works of earlier anti-essentialist black writers, such as Fanon. Henry Louis Gates Jr. is a prominent figure, in both academic and wider circles, within this current. 'Race is the ultimate trope of difference', Gates writes, 'because it is so very arbitrary in its application. The biological criteria used to determine "difference" in sex simply do not hold when applied to "race"' (1985, p. 5).

In opposition to such views, another African American critic, Joyce Joyce (1987, p. 341), accuses Gates and those who concur with him of aligning themselves with an anti-Black perspective. 'It is insidious', she writes, 'for the Black literary critic to adopt any kind of strategy that diminishes or ... negates his blackness.' Picking her way through this debate Fuss (1989) makes the following point on white critics' readiness to treat race as a kind of social fantasy:

> In American culture, 'race' has been far more an acknowledged component of black identity than white; for good or bad, whites have always seen 'race' as a minority attribute, and blacks have courageously and persistently agitated on behalf of

'the race'. It is easy enough for white poststructuralist critics to place under erasure something that they think they never had to begin with.

(ibid., p. 93)

Baker has reached a similar conclusion about the tendency among contemporary scientists to denounce racial discourse as unscientific, and hence irrational:

The scenario they seem to endorse reads as follows: when science apologises and says there is no such thing [as race], all talk of 'race' must cease. Hence, 'race', as a recently emergent, unifying, and forceful sign of difference *in the service* of the 'Other', is held up to scientific ridicule as, ironically, 'unscientific'. A proudly emergent sense of ethnic diversity in the service of new world arrangements is disparaged by white male science as the most foolish sort of anachronism.

(1986, p. 186)

However, although Fuss and Baker are clearly right to address certain ironies in the development of anti-essentialist anti-racism, the practical implications of their hostility are more difficult to gauge. Should we, could we, for political reasons, pretend that race is, in fact, a fixed essence, while knowing full well that it is not? The stance known as 'strategic essentialism' seems to offer this possibility. For, in the eyes of some critics, the gulf between essentialist and anti-essentialist positions may be bridged by the development of 'a strategic use of positivist essentialism, in a scrupulous visible political interest' (Spivak, cited by Fuss, 1989, p. 187). Such a position appears to enable minority groups to preserve identities that facilitate struggle, resistance and solidarity while maintaining a critique of reified notions of race. Asked to expand on the implications of strategic essentialism, the term's progenitor, Spivak, comments, 'The only way to work with collective agency is to teach a persistent critique of collective agency at the same time ... It is a persistent critique of what one cannot not want' (1990, p. 93). The allusion to '*what one cannot*

not want' indicates Spivak's conviction that essentialism cannot be removed from political discourse, that politics relies on fictions of identity. Fuss addresses the same point in her critique of the way anti-essentialist perspectives tend to be selective as to *which* essences are deconstructed. Fuss claims that the notion of 'the social', and the related relativist idea of 'social location', are often untouched within anti-essentialist discourse. She finds that

> the strength of the constructionist position is its rigorous insistence on the production of social categories like 'the body' and its attention to systems of representation. But this strength is not built on the grounds of essentialism's demise, rather it works its power by strategically deferring the encounter with essence, displacing it.
>
> (1989, p. 6)

As this suggests, anti-essentialism is, at some point, reliant on essentialism: the encounter with essentialism can be deferred but never entirely avoided. However, this is not to suggest that the two strategies are equivalent. For while anti-essentialism is a reflexive tendency, an attempt to question taken-for-granted categories and experiences, essentialism leads away from reflexivity; it is a tendency that tries to close down political debate and sustain existing notions and labels. If we accept this formulation, then, although we may concur that the tension between anti-essentialism and essentialism is not amenable to clear or final resolution, we should be prepared to admit that the former is the more creative and intellectually open of the two currents. This position suggests a prescriptive conclusion: that anti-essentialism should be a privileged discourse within anti-racism; it may be unobtainable but it needs to be reached for.

ANTI-RACISM AND WHITE IDENTITIES

Anti-racists have often placed the critique of the racial attitudes and dominance of white people at the centre of their project. Yet white people have also played a role *within* anti-racism, as critics and as activists. In order to explore the problematic role of whites in anti-racism I will look first of all at notions of whiteness within anti-racism before reviewing some recent interventions that have attempted to make the issue of whiteness more legible. As we shall see, within the new area of 'white studies' we can find the possibility of more historically and theoretically sophisticated anti-racist readings of whiteness.

How obvious is it that this book has been written by a white person? I have left it until now to admit it. Many readers will, no doubt, have 'worked it out' some time ago. But how could that have been done? And what exactly am I confessing to? Whiteness is, after all, a peculiar identity. It appears to be both everywhere and nowhere, simultaneously a pervasive normative presence and an invisible, largely undiscussed, absence. As Judith Levine (1994, p. 11) notes, whiteness is 'the standard against which the Other is inferior, like the moon from a moving car – it remains ever the same, untouchable, yet right outside the window'.

The 'untouchability' of whiteness has also been a characteristic of anti-racist debate in Western countries. This is not, of course, to suggest that the supposed attributes of white racial conscious-ness have not been examined by anti-racists (for they have; see, for example, Katz, 1978; Wellman, 1977). It is, however, to observe that whiteness has tended to be approached by anti-racists as a fixed, asocial category rather than something with a history or geography. In other words, anti-racists have, for the most part, yet to become aware of, and escape from, the practice of treating whiteness as a static, ahistorical, aspatial 'thing': something set outside social change, something that defines the 'other' but is not itself subject to others' definitions.

Such rigid constructions of whiteness may serve specific strategic purposes in anti-racist struggles. However, they also appear to have other consequences for race equality initiatives and research. They lead towards the positioning (or self-positioning) of white people as fundamentally outside, and untouched by, the contemporary controversies of racial identity politics. They lead to white people being allowed to understand whiteness as an unproblematic category (albeit with negative attributes), a category which is not subject to the constant processes of challenge and change experienced by non-white groups. This process enables white people to occupy a privileged location in anti-racist debate; they are allowed the luxury of being passive observers, of being altruistically motivated, of knowing that their racial identity might be reviled and lambasted but never actually made slippery, torn open, or, indeed, abolished.

The focus of the new area of race scholarship known as 'white studies' is upon the racialisation process that produces whiteness. The political problematic of writers and activists within this, mainly North American, group, is how this process may be simultaneously identified and challenged. However, there exists considerable diversity within this school. Two broad tendencies may be discerned. The first attempts to subsume the analysis of whiteness within a class analysis of racialisation. The second stresses the plural constitution, and multiple lived experiences of whiteness. These approaches may also be distinguished in terms of the role they assign ethnicity. In what has become a traditional radical argument, Marxists within white studies have aligned the assertion of white ethnicities to a conservative, depoliticising multiculturalism. Thus their strategy demands that a 'whites versus blacks' model of race is sustained, denaturalised and politicised. By contrast, writing and research that have focused on the 'white experience' have been more receptive to the possibility that ethnicity can act to deconstruct the homogenising monolith of whiteness.

Theodore Allen (1994) and David Roediger (1992, 1994), and the contributors to the journal *Race Traitor* (the journal's subtitle: *Treason to Whiteness is Loyalty to Humanity*), may be placed firmly within the former camp. Each traces whiteness as a project of American capitalism and labour organisations and each explicitly calls for its 'abolition'. This group views white identity as the creation of racialised capitalism, as an ideology that offers false rewards to one racialised faction of the working class at the expense of others. Thus, it is argued that the task of anti-racists is not to encourage white people to confess to their 'own identity' but to enable them to politically and historically contextualise, then to resist and abandon, whiteness. The editors of *Race Traitor* explain their project in the following terms: 'Two points define the position of *Race Traitor*: first, that the "white race" is not a natural but a historical category; second, that what was historically constructed can be undone' (1994, p. 108). The focus of research for this group has been upon the entry of European heritage immigrants in the USA into a racialised labour market, more specifically their ability to situate themselves as part of white labour and be distinguished from non-white labour. In *How the Irish Became White* (Ignatiev, 1995), *The Invention of the White Race* (Allen, 1994) and Roediger's two books, *The Wages of Whiteness* (1992) and *Towards the Abolition of Whiteness* (1994), this process is shown to have subverted working-class solidarity and reproduced the position of whiteness as the axis of ruling class power. Ignatiev and many of the contributors to *Race Traitor* emphasise that resistance to this process entails white people's abandonment of 'loyalty' to the 'white club', a process that they see as enabling class consciousness to finally emerge from behind the distortive ideologies of race. Reflecting their conviction that loyalty to whiteness is equated by state agencies with loyalty to the economic and political status quo, Garvey and Ignatiev ask:

> What would happen if the police could not discern a loyal person by color alone? What if there were enough people who looked white but were really enemies of the official society, so the cops did not know whom to beat and whom to leave alone? ... At the present time, the class bias of the law is partially repressed by racial considerations, and the removal of those considerations would give it free rein ... European Americans of the downtrodden class would at last be compelled to face their real conditions of life and their relations with humankind. It would be the end of the white race and the beginning of a new phase in the struggle for a better world.
>
> (1997, p. 348)

Despite the reference to 'a better world', Ignatiev (1997) has elsewhere noted that this project is designed for and only applies to the USA. In fact, the obsessive focus on that country within the 'white studies' debate has meant that its participants appear unaware that the loosening of individuals' 'loyalty' to whiteness has occurred in many societies in the twentieth century (for example, within Latin America, see Bonnett, 1999) without the collapse of 'official society'. Indeed, a more international frame of reference brings into visibility the association of whiteness with modernity, rather than simply capitalism and, by extension, is suggestive of the complicity of Marxism and class reductionism with Eurocentrism.

Another aspect of *Race Traitor*'s approach that a wider and more international context reveals is the implications that flow from placing non-whiteness outside 'official society'. More specifically, there exists within this body of work a persistent romanticisation of blackness. Indeed, *Race Traitor*'s project is not merely to destroy whiteness but to enable whites to 'assimilate' blackness. Of course, blackness too is seen as a social construction. But it is construed as a construction that needs to be supported and reproduced. The editors argue that

> when whites reject their racial identity, they take a big step towards becoming human. But may that step not entail, for many, some engagement with blackness, perhaps even an identification as 'black'? Recent experience, in this country and elsewhere, would indicate that it does.
>
> (*Race Traitor*, 1994, p. 115)

This formulation is clearly based upon a series of assumptions concerning the meaning of blackness. It implies that the romantic stereotype of the eternally resisting, victimised 'black community' is required to be further strengthened in order to create a suitable location for escapees from whiteness. Thus black people are condemned to racial stereotype as the price of white people's liberation.

Those contributors to 'white studies' more concerned with elucidating the paradoxes of 'white experience' than class politics

have tried to provide a more complex account of its social constitution. In particular Ruth Frankenberg's study *The Social
Construction of Whiteness* (1993) provides a number of insights into
the slippery, incomplete, and diverse nature of white racial identity. Frankenberg draws from her interviews with thirty white
Californian women a complex portrait of '[the] articulations of
whiteness, seeking to specify how each is marked by the interlocking effects of geographical origin, generation, ethnicity,
political orientation, gender and present-day geographical location' (ibid., p. 18).

Frankenberg's attention to the intersecting nature of identities
is translated into depictions of how different types of white
people engage with whiteness. Thus her respondents are introduced through potted biographies which are filtered by
Frankenberg to provide certain key categories of experience that
determine or shape their attitudes towards race. This approach
attempts to combine highly individual context with generalised
accounts of the nature of, for example, 'lesbian', 'Jewish', 'middle-
class' experience. The tension between these two types of
knowledge is cohered and concealed in Frankenberg's account
both by references to the 'complexity' of experience and to a
prescriptive political strategy of 'naming' whiteness. The latter
approach relies on the contention that making whiteness visible
can undermine its normative power. Thus, in contrast to the
ambition to abolish whiteness associated with the *Race Traitor*
school, Frankenberg suggests that white people's whiteness
should be 'outed'. Only when it has been 'admitted to' can it be
confronted. 'Naming whiteness and white people in this sense',
she notes, 'helps dislodge the claims of both to rightful dominance' (1993, p. 234).

The confessional implications of Frankenberg's position are
suggestive of its inability to escape one of the central paradoxes of
anti-racist history, that escape from racism has so often been by
way of racialisation. This is also true of the interest in hybrid or
cross-over identities that Frankenberg shares with others in the
field. In particular, her work invokes parallels with the creative
appropriation and inter-mixing of ethnic identities observed by a

number of commentators of contemporary youth cultures (for example, Hebdige, 1979; Jones, 1989). For example, in Simon Jones's (1989) ethnographic study of white Rastafarians in Birmingham, a 'white community' is portrayed that self-consciously splices its own whiteness with styles and ideologies associated with Rastafarianism. This escape, as Jones notes, draws on a correlation of whiteness with boredom and passivity and of blackness with rebellion and the exotic. It is an 'escape', then, based on certain familiar clichés of whiteness and blackness (see also Rubio, 1993). Nevertheless, despite this reliance, the process of becoming and socially interacting as a white Rastafarian does appear from Jones's account to open up the racialisation process, creating incomplete, impermanent and explicitly constructed moments of appropriation and cultural play.

However, the 'confusion', and mixing, of racial signs and boundaries are not restricted to moments of youthful transgression. Disruptive and mutant forms of white identity have a long and varied lineage. For example, Roediger (1992, 1994) draws attention to the ambivalent inclusion within and exclusion from whiteness of Irish and Italian immigrants within the USA in the nineteenth century. Roediger (forthcoming) has also contributed a related essay on the development of the categories 'Guinea' and 'Wigger' in the same country. Each of these two terms denotes a racial classification that fuses, and to some extent transcends, notions of white and black. 'Guinea' was used in the late nineteenth century as a collective noun for Italian immigrants, African Americans and certain 'mestizo' populations. The slang word 'wigger' (a contraction of 'white nigger'), which retains a certain currency within North American racial nomenclature, was formulated at about the same time as a slur on those whites who were deemed to be 'acting black'. Over recent years, however, its meaning has become less clearly derogatory. Indeed, as Roediger notes, Wigger is today 'used approvingly by white would-be hiphoppers to describe each other'.

Histories of the complex and plural formations of whiteness are a useful resource for any anti-racist engagement with white identity. However, the ambiguity of whiteness may also be located on a more fundamental level. The implication of a number of psychoanalytically informed studies of the 'chronic instability of the binaries constructed in colonial discourse' (Rattansi, 1994, p. 39) is that even if one ignores the transgressive youth or ethnic borderlands of Western identities, and focuses on the 'centre' or 'heartlands' of whiteness, one will discover racialised subjectivities that, far from being settled and confident, exhibit a constantly reformulated panic over the meaning of whiteness and the defining presence of non-whiteness within it. To provide a concise illustration of this process we may turn to the novel by Darius James (1993), *Negrophobia*. The book attempts to open up the racist imagination of its central character, a white girl called Bubbles Brazil. It relates how Bubbles's horror of all things non-white reflects the centrality of 'non-whiteness' (more specifically, blackness) to her own identity. Bubbles, whose father was a Black and White Minstrel, whose most delirious childhood games were escapes from whiteness into phantasms of blackness, demands and perpetuates non-whiteness as an essential part of her sense of self. By the novel's conclusion Bubbles's whiteness is revealed as a desperate and somewhat ragged manufacture; a continually failing exercise to reject and repel those fantasies of otherness that animate and shape it.

CONCLUSION

The four dilemmas discussed in this chapter provide further evidence of the complex and often contradictory nature of anti-racism. Rattansi (1992, pp. 52–53) argues that 'If anti-racism is to be effective', it will be 'necessary to take a hard and perhaps painful look at the terms under which [it has] operated so far'. More specifically, Rattansi calls attention to anti-racists' inadequate and simplistic modes of racial representation. Apparently unprepared to acknowledge the 'contradictions, inconsistencies and ambivalences' (ibid., p. 73) within white and non-white identities, anti-racism (or at least the contemporary British radical variety towards which Rattansi's criticism appears directed) can often appear ill equipped to engage with the fluid and complex forces of the racialisation process.

However, the danger I alluded to at the start of this chapter needs to be borne in mind. For posing dilemmas for anti-racism can lead, if we are not careful, to a simplistic and linear conception of anti-racist history. In other words, it encourages us to fabricate an ordered, conveniently sequential narrative in which 'dilemmas' are followed by 'resolutions'. Moreover, it makes us forget that the nature and content of anti-racist debate vary geographically, not merely from nation to nation but from region to region, place to place. Indeed, one of the unfortunate consequences of a narrow, chronological view of anti-racist debate is that it appears to demand that a spatial centre be found for the development and dissemination of what are inevitably construed as the most 'advanced' currents within the discussion. Thus it is imagined that provincial places are forever 'behind' in 'The Debate'. From the 'West', more specifically from places like Paris or New York, the 'new ideas' are seen to emerge. Out in the non-Western world or the margins of Western countries, 'they have never heard of' white studies, 'they are still talking about' race as if it really existed ... they try to catch up, but the centre is always ahead of the game.

Such a perspective encourages us to overlook three things: the way different national or regional communities of anti-racists have their own set of dilemmas; the fact that dilemma is intrinsic to anti-racist debate; and, finally, that anti-racism is part and parcel of wider processes of socio-economic change. We find clear examples of all these traits in anti-racist debate in many Latin American societies. Despite the fact that Western aid agencies have encouraged the adoption of Western-style anti-racism in South and Central American countries, these societies have their own histories of anti-racist struggle. To construct, say, anti-essentialism as the 'latest', most 'advanced', response to some recent 'crisis' in anti-racism casts the debate over *mestizaje* as marginalia, a footnote to the real controversies as defined in Europe or North America. Moreover, although it may be easier to narrate a transition from one ideology to another by reference to the contributions of gifted individuals ('Modood challenges racial dualism', 'Spivak introduces strategic essentialism', and so on), anti-racist ideas are not simply a product of intellectual discussion but also of economic and social processes. Thus, for example, the transition from modern to post-modern capitalism in Latin America may help explain why more plural, less fixed, notions of identity are currently being favoured and the solidarities of mass identity, especially mass political identity, are being cast as 'old-fashioned' (indeed, as 'dilemmas' that require 'solution').

The dilemmas identified in this chapter are real and important ones within anti-racist debate. But I would caution readers to view them not as stepping stones on a straight and clear path, but as points of dispute within a wide and varied landscape of social change.

5

ANTI-ANTI-RACISM?

INTRODUCTION

This chapter introduces criticism of anti-racism. More specifically, it addresses the objections that have been raised to anti-racism from those who position themselves as on the left or on the right of the political spectrum.

The number of societies where a 'backlash' against racial equity is, or has been, evident is considerable. However, the most explicit and debated challenges to anti-racism are to be found within Western countries. And it is upon these societies, more especially the USA and Britain in the 1980s and early 1990s, that this chapter will focus (see also Gabriel, 1998). In these countries, and during these years, criticism of anti-racism gathered pace to the extent that we may speak of the emergence of 'anti-anti-racism', a tendency with sufficient power to shape the way people understand what anti-racism actually is. Within Britain, towards the end of the 1990s, this explicit hostility abated. However, by that time anti-racism had been reduced to a marginal current within public sector provision. The anti-anti-racists had, in this area at least, won. As a consequence, anti-racism's 'return to favour' in the late 1990s was characterised by the absence of connections to, and knowledge of, the debates and practices of the past. As this implies, the following study may be read as illustrative of the way hostility to anti-racism can erupt into view, disrupting the development of opposition to racism and severing its historical memory.

Although this chapter is structured around a distinction between left-wing and right-wing opinion, the debate on anti-racism has, perhaps more than any other, demonstrated the overlapping and interlocking nature of these constituencies. Claims to oppose 'Eurocentrism' seem to get under the skin of defenders of both the European heritage of socialism and the European heritage of conservatism. Both position anti-racism as a force that *fragments*, that weakens and disperses. As this suggests, both forms of critique fail to register the fact that anti-racism and its antecedents have existed within and through 'their traditions' for centuries. Both radical and conservative hostility to anti-racism arise from highly strategic readings of the historical record. Thus, while Marxists often hark back to a time when class politics was undisturbed by, or could comfortably assimilate, divisions of class and ethnicity, conservative commentators conjure an equally untroubled past of cultural consensus. Such accounts are more reliable as reflections of a contemporary 'back-lash' against race and ethnic equality than as windows into the past.

Moreover, although left-wing and right-wing critics exhibit different political priorities, they both have something else in common, namely a narrow view of anti-racist history and geography. More specifically, anti-racism is routinely understood as a recent phenomenon, as confined to North America or Britain, and as driven by nothing more substantive than fashion and conceit. As this implies, all these critics tend to be engaged in very particular, and often highly instrumental, interventions: anti-racism/multiculturalism is construed as a superficial and discrete political agenda that can be humiliated or defeated.

Indeed, we may speak of these critiques creating a stereotype of anti-racism, establishing a cliché or image that subverts the possibility of establishing less parochial and more informed debate on the topic.

The following chapter should be read more as a case study in resistance to anti-racism, than as a comprehensive survey of anti-anti-racism. The latter project would be almost as ambitious as the whole of the present book. The attacks on anti-racism discussed here originated in particular times and particular countries. And, as mentioned, they are orientated towards very particular definitions of what anti-racism is. Wider interpretations of anti-racism, as a theme with deep and broad roots in Western and non-Western societies, are almost invariably ignored by these critics, a practice that enables their polemical, often angry, tone. The characteristic mocking belligerence of these critics may also explain their tendency to fail to notice their complicity with the object of their derision. For if we accept that anti-racism is a fundamental facet of twentieth-century history, a social process embedded in the formation of modern nations, capitalism and social movements, then claims to oppose it begin to look very muddled; indeed, as reactionary to the point of eccentricity. In fact the secret history of many self-proclaimed critics of anti-racism is their acceptance of many of its most basic claims.

THE RIGHT VERSUS ANTI-RACISM

Anti-racism is not intrinsically left-wing or anti-capitalist. Indeed, it may and often has been accommodated within free-market ideologies. However, politically motivated critics of anti-racism tend to approach it as a discrete phenomenon, associated with shockingly novel equity initiatives. And, for many on the right, these initiatives are firmly associated with a liberal or left-wing political agenda.

It is important to note that anti-anti-racism is not an entirely original development within conservative politics. Within Britain, for example, what may be termed 'anti-anti-colonialism' was an early incarnation of the right's opposition to attacks on European racism. This hostility to anti-colonialism was often characterised by the attempt to portray the anti-colonial movement as extremist, authoritarian and a form of reverse discrimination (because it was 'anti-white'). One race expert attached to the Colonial Office, Sir Alan Burns, explained in 1959 that 'in many cases "anti-colonialism" was merely a cover for intense racial feeling, a colour prejudice in reverse' (cited by Füredi, 1998, p. 203).

The same wing of the British Conservative Party associated with recent anti-anti-racism, namely its right-wing (i.e. its highly patriotic and *laissez-faire* orientated wing), was also the most closely associated with anti-anti-colonialism. Thus, for example, in *Africa: Hope Deferred* (1972) the Conservative MP John Biggs-Davison assailed the intemperate, prejudiced, and anti-white nature of anti-colonialism (including opposition to apartheid). Biggs-Davison portrayed African independence as an economic and social disaster. 'It is said', he remarks, 'that many Congolese plaintively ask: "When will this Independence end?"' (ibid., p. 94).

However, although anti-anti-racism may be seen as a tendency with a long and, as yet, uncharted history, its most explicit incarnations are relatively recent. As befits a debate with narrow historical horizons, the interventions of anti-anti-racists have already been judged by some a success. Gilroy (1990) writing in the wake of British government attacks on municipal anti-racism wrote of the 'end of anti-racism'. When set against the vast role and range of anti-racist tendencies within modern culture, such a statement may appear bizarre. However, it needs to be understood as the product of an intensive period of political activism and reaction around the issue of racism. Anti-racist agendas were asserted with increasing visibility from the 1950s in the USA, and late 1960s in Britain. Opposition to these agendas accompanied them every step of the way. In Britain, for example, the Race Relations Act of 1968 was bitterly opposed by many on the right. Articulating a sentiment common to later conservative criticism, Enoch Powell (1969) called the Act 'reverse discrimination'. It 'is not the immigrant but the Briton', Powell claimed, 'who [now] feels himself the "toad beneath the harrow"' (ibid., p. 301).

Conservative critics of anti-racism have tended to construe it as 'extreme'. This notion is, in part, explicable by reference to the polemical nature of anti-anti-racism, i.e. it tends towards exaggeration, and the use of emotive 'extreme cases' as if they were representative of all anti-racist work. Thus, for example, the contributors to the volume *Anti-racism: An Assault on Education and Value* (Palmer, 1986) return again and again to the Marxist anti-racism of the private research group, the Institute of Race Relations, to illustrate what is wrong with all anti-racism. However, just as it is misleading to collapse anti-racism into Marxist revolution, so it is erroneous to conflate all right-wing criticism. For a number of differences of perspective can be detected, the most fundamental of which is between those conservatives who oppose anti-racism because they associate it with state intervention and interference and those conservatives who oppose it because they do not like or want a society that threatens the dominance of Western values and/or people. The distinction is a significant one because it exposes a significant split in mainstream right-wing thinking between social egalitarians and anti-egalitarians. These two camps and the associated tensions between them exist within most modern conservative movements and political parties. The example I shall use here, of the British Conservative government's attacks on anti-racism in the 1980s and early 1990s, evidences the attitude of both groups.

The British Conservative Party includes a diversity of opinion on anti-racism. There are those within the party who have been content to offer support for anti-racism and, indeed, to see the state intervene to maintain a sustainable multiracial society. Those who may be cast as anti-anti-racists fall into, or straddle, the two camps mentioned above, i.e. those who are opposed to anti-racism because they see it as inherently interventionist and contrary to their *laissez-faire* principles and those who oppose it because they construe the idea of anti-racism as a subversion of British culture. For the latter group it often appears as if anti-racism is, in and of itself, offensive, while for the former anti-racism is simply not seen as the 'job of the state'.

Under the leadership of Margaret Thatcher these two strands gained greater authority within the party and were able to influence, if never entirely dominate, government policy. The two themes were brought together, and the tension between them concealed, by an emphasis on the *unnecessary and unwanted* nature of anti-racism. These themes relied, in turn, on a very particular construct of anti-racism as the creation of 'hard left', recklessly profligate, local governments. An even more particular symbol was central to this attack, that of the so-called 'loony left' public professional. This last menace to both British capitalism and British tradition was employed as a 'hate figure' that integrated the concerns of the *laissez-faire* and nationalist, socially conservative, tendencies within Conservative politics.

Introducing a package of educational reforms designed, in part, to sweep away the influence of anti-racism, Margaret Thatcher told a Conservative Party conference in 1987 that young people's opportunity for a 'decent education ... is all too often snatched from them by hard-left education authorities and extremist teachers. Children who need to be able to count and multiply are learning anti-racist mathematics, whatever that may be' (quoted by Tomlinson, 1990, p. 90).

The abolition of the two local authorities that had the most high-profile anti-racist policies in the United Kingdom, the Greater London Council and the Inner London Education Authority, in 1986 and 1990, respectively, provides one of the more striking manifestations of the Conservatives' determination to root out anti-racism from local politics (see also Ball and Solomos, 1990). However, the most far-reaching measure introduced to stymie anti-racism was the 1988 Education Reform Act. Signalling its departure from traditional educational goals the Secretary of State for Education, Kenneth Baker (1987, p. 9), introduced this piece of legislation at the 1987 Conservative Party Annual Conference with the words, 'the pursuit of egalitarianism is now over'. The Act's two most important features attempted to both by-pass and undermine that branch of government that had become associated with the development of equity initiatives in education, local education authorities. More specifically, administration of schools was passed as far as possible to school governors (who tend to be more concerned with day-to-day management than wider social issues). In addition, a National Curriculum was created with a nationalist pedagogic remit. Thus, for example, one senior official at the School Curriculum and Assessment Authority (Tate, 1994, p. 10) explained that the 'proposals for British history, a Standard English and the English literary heritage are designed to reinforce a common culture'.

These Conservative initiatives were supported by the British press. Indeed, a high-profile campaign against anti-racism continued throughout the 1980s in nearly all British national newspapers (Murray, 1986; Gordon, 1990). The two central themes that were developed within this campaign were that, a) anti-racism is a product of the extreme left, and b) that anti-racism is anti-white and anti-British. These themes were generally presented in the language of ridicule, a stance encapsulated in the name the press gave to anti-racists – the 'loony left'. The tone of derision was also evident in the kind of news items about anti-racism the press chose to highlight. Nancy Murray (1986) provides us with an example concerning anti-racists' supposed desire to ban Tufty the Squirrel:

> over fifty articles sending up the left – some a full page long – appeared in the national and regional press when there was an alleged leak from Lambeth Council that it was about to ban its road safety symbol, Tufty the Squirrel, on the grounds that it was both 'racist and sexist'. The fact that the story was bogus did not deter the papers, which found Tufty irresistible.
>
> (ibid., p. 8)

Other loony-left stories appeared in connection with the alleged banning, by left-wing local authorities, of the nursery rhyme 'Baa Baa Black Sheep', along with black garbage bags and all reference to black coffee in staff canteens. Anti-anti-racist news items, repeated almost every day in one of the mass circulation newspapers, had a profound effect on the image of anti-racism. Anti-racism became a political liability. Sikora (1988, p. 52) reports one official in a local authority in the North West of England admitting that 'to openly declare itself anti-racist the Authority might suffer the consequences of being branded "left-wing" and "extremist" and experience ... negative treatment from the media'. In the early 1990s the notion of 'political correctness', imported from the North American media, re-ignited this discourse of derision. However, it is indicative of how successful anti-anti-racism had been that the examples of British 'political correctness' located were often of a rather insubstantial variety. Indeed, *The Sunday Times* (22 January 1995) found itself reduced to announcing that Haringey was the 'Barmiest Borough in Britain' – and the most 'politically correct' – on the basis of such evidence as, to quote the newspaper's staccato outrage, '*Daddy's Roommate*, a book on what it is like to have gay parents, placed in children's libraries'.

The right-wing assault on 'anti-racism' may be judged, in part at least, to have achieved its aims. The target of the attack – namely local authority-funded anti-racist programmes – fell out of favour in the 1980s and 1990s not merely with Conservatives, but for the three largest political parties in Britain. This 'victory over anti-racism' has parallels with the backlash against multicul-turalism and affirmative action in the USA. In particular, so-called 'reverse discrimination' has become the fulcrum of a debate that has called into question the very notion of assistance, state or otherwise, for disadvantaged sections of society. As this implies, the attacks mounted on multiculturalism and affirmative action are characterised, not by an interest in developing alterna-tive ways that the state or private business might create racial equality (cf. Kahlenberg, 1995), but by an antagonism to the very idea that equality can or should be socially engineered. Reflecting the conservative mood, in an article entitled 'Is affir-mative action doomed?', Rosen (1994, p. 26) depicted race-preference policies as 'the most extreme form of racialism'. Richard Kahlenberg noted in 1995 (p. 21) that 'As the country's mood swings violently against affirmative action ... the whole project of legislating racial equality seems suddenly in doubt. The Democrats, terrified of the issue, are now hoping it will just go away.'

The themes drawn out below all testify to the particularity of right-wing critics' understanding of the anti-racist tradition. For them anti-racism is the product of progressive or left-wing politics. It is, moreover, something epiphenomenal to Western culture: it is seen to have been born sometime in the very recent past, and to have illegitimately seized hold of certain institutions. It is implied throughout this body of criticism that if we got rid of anti-racism, few would miss it. Moreover, society would function all the better for its absence. Ironically, these critics also tend to be adamant not merely that they are not racists, but that racism must be opposed, and that Western society must be defended precisely because it is based on principles of tolerance, equality and liberty. As we shall see, it is one of the ironies of conservative anti-anti-racism that it demonises anti-racism so completely that it appears unable to come to terms with its operation within its own discourse.

Exposing the myth of Western racism

The notion that anti-racists view Western society as entirely racist and non-Western society as entirely non- or anti-racist, is central to much right-wing criticism. Opposing this imagined perspective these critics defend Western society as tolerant and humane. In certain versions of this thesis Western culture is held to be more advanced than other cultures precisely because it adheres to principles of liberty and universal rights. As this implies, this critique contains the danger of slipping into contradiction: of attacking anti-racism while celebrating Western society as anti-racist. This problem is, in part, resolved by viewing anti-racism as a distinct, authoritarian and intolerant tradition. Anti-racists are portrayed as people who like to impose their will on others. For O'Keefe (1986) anti-racism reflects the 'totalitarian politics of persuasion' (ibid., p. 191) and the 'old socialist desire to push others around, to decide what is good for them' (ibid., p. 194). In an essay entitled 'Anti-racism versus freedom' Lewis asserts that anti-racism is an alien cuckoo in the nest of Western tolerance: 'simple appeals to our sense of justice, from anti-racists, as from Marxists, may mask sinister and subversive aims' (1988, p. 137).

Right-wing critics often attempt to turn the tables on anti-racism by suggesting that anti-racism could only ever have flowered within a tolerant, diverse society, like the West. In this narrative anti-racism is represented as a kind of extreme, self-hating, mutant creation of Western liberty. 'Multicultural demands in American schools and universities', noted D'Souza (1995) in *The End of Racism*:

> arise from the conviction that Western culture is constitutively defined by a virtually uninterrupted series of crimes visited upon other groups. ... Non-Western cultures have virtually no indigenous tradition of equality ... the Western attitude of tolerance finds itself confronted with the cultural reality of non-Western intolerance.
>
> (ibid., pp. 357–358)

Authentic Western tolerance is aligned by D'Souza with a benign universalism. In similar vein, in his essay, 'The mythology of British racism', O'Keefe (1986) asserts that the glory of British culture is its disposition against prejudice. Anti-racism, he notes, is merely a 'flood of self-hatred', a form of masochistic 'self-abasement' (ibid., p. 187). Of course, as I have already indicated, this line of reasoning necessarily inserts right-wing critics within the cultural current they wish to attack: presenting themselves as the voices of real tolerance, they locate themselves, albeit inadvertently, as the 'real anti-racists'. And yet these writers appear uninterested in articulating anti-racism in conservative terms, only in demolishing it. As this implies, and given the nature and tone of their attacks, it may be ventured that their claims to be motivated by a desire to uphold traditions of Western tolerance are unsustainable. Indeed, at least some of these critical contributions can be placed within pre- or ante-Enlightenment traditions of ethnic insularity. For there remains a persistent tendency within the more nationalistic and patriotic currents of this body of work to assert that it is natural for people to racially and culturally 'stick to their own'. For Roger Scruton (cited by Gordon and Klug, 1986, p. 14) explains that 'illiberal sentiments ... arise inevitably from social consciousness: they involve natural prejudice, and a desire for the company of one's own kind'. The notion that anti-racism is pitting itself against 'human nature' and, hence, represents a doomed and utopian project emerges time and again in 'new right' critics. It is a current that highlights the fragility of this group's claims on 'the Enlightenment tradition' of political citizenship and legal equality. It seems that, for at least some of its critics, the claim that anti-racism 'could only ever have been born in the West' is of less concern than the fact that it offends primordial instincts of blood and kin.

Opposing the 'race industry'

> [They] prattle incessantly about inclusiveness, diversity and multiculturalism ... for the oldest of reasons: they want power and money.
>
> (Warder, 1993, p. 655)

Right-wing anti-anti-racism often mirrors the critiques developed by more sympathetic observers. However, while the latter's criticism is designed to change anti-racism, the former's is employed to rid society of it. This pattern is seen particularly clearly in the attacks both sympathetic and hostile commentators have made against the development of a so-called 'race industry'. For many radical critics, such as Gilroy (1987b), the formation of 'anti-racist bureaucracies' is indicative of anti-racism's alienation from the concerns of ordinary black people and a sign of the recuperation of 'black struggle' by a 'black petite bourgeoisie' (ibid., p. 13). Yet, while both conservative and radical critics have criticised the development of hierarchical and authoritarian anti-racist bureaucracies, with little contact with the groups they claim to represent and with a vested interest in identifying social problems as racial ones, right-wing criticism has tended to assume that these characteristics are inevitable within anti-racism. This assumption necessarily relies on a vision of anti-racism as a very particular, and not a little bizarre, mind-set; a kind of sub-culture with its own fixed codes and expectations. Indeed, a favoured conservative metaphor for anti-racist activists is that of the cult or sect. Construing anti-racism as a 'new doctrine', the British educationalist Ray Honeyford (1986) goes on to identify it with a clan of blinkered extremists, who employ the word 'racist' to strengthen group solidarity:

> A 'racist' is to the race relations lobby what 'Protestant' was to the inquisitors of the Counter-Reformation, or 'witches' was to the seventeenth-century burghers of Salem. It is the totem of the new doctrine of anti-racism. Its definition varies according to the purpose it is meant to achieve. It is a gift to the zealot, since he can apply it to anyone who disagrees with him – and he often ejaculates the word as though it were a synonym for 'rapist' or 'fascist'. It takes its force not from its power to describe but from its power to coerce and intimidate. It is attached to anyone who challenges the arguments or rhetoric of the race relations lobby.
>
> (ibid., p. 51)

The assumption that anti-racists are involved in the racialising of society follows from Honeyford's depiction. As we saw in the previous chapter, racialisation is an issue of continuing debate within anti-racism. However, for right-wing critics it appears as an inescapable consequence of anti-racism. Again and again in such commentary the assumption is made that talking about racial inequality creates racial tension, and that racism and racial difference would not be so important, or indeed exist, if the anti-racist lobby were not there to 'stir things up'. For Andrew Alexander writing in the *Daily Mail*:

> We have thus now reached the stage where the official and not just the unofficial parts of the race relations industry have one overriding aim: to make us all eat, breathe and sleep 'race' ... For though the race relations industry may not have succeeded in improving race relations — it has made them vastly more prickly and vastly worse — it has succeeded brilliantly in one thing: making people dead scared of the accusation of being 'racially prejudiced'.
>
> (24 October 1983)

Similarly, for Palmer, 'those whose profession it is to combat racial conflict have a vested interest in promoting it' (1986, p. 82). Marks concurs: 'the hidden agenda of the anti-racists' includes the adoption of policies, practices and attitudes which increase polarisation, heighten racial tensions and make racial conflict more probable' (1986, p. 33). The assertion that anti-racism is a form of insurgency which promotes 'racial tensions' represents one of the most extreme forms of conservative anti-anti-racism. It is, moreover, a perspective indicative of a particular moment in British anti-racism in the mid-1980s, a period when conservatives were seeking and gaining control over the welfare system. It is noticeable that, when the issue of the need for anti-racist education and training resurfaced in the British media (in 1999, following a racist murder; see Macpherson, 1999), the voices of opposition, although still well represented in the press, were more isolated and received far less support from the leadership of the Conservative Party. In part this may be explained by the fact that by 1999, the struggle over education appeared over. The 'back-to-basics', Conservative, education agenda had been accepted by the Labour Government. Hence, anti-racism was no longer so easily imagined as the harbinger of leftist revolt. Rather, it was widely construed as part and parcel of a practical and consensus-building approach to state provision. The content of the proposed anti-racist initiatives was, by and large, the same as those of their, much reviled, predecessors. It was their *role as a site of political struggle* that had changed.

Racial equality and the free market

The assertion that anti-racism is foreign to, and an unwelcome intrusion within, the free market forms a core principle of much right-wing opposition. Within this perspective anti-racism is construed as interventionist, its power emanating either from the state or from anti-capitalist interest groups who have managed to unduly influence the corporate sector. Reflecting its *laissez-faire* orientation this viewpoint tends to posit racial inequality as a bad thing, but a bad thing that the free market can overcome and which government anti-racism only makes worse. As this suggests, this form of right-wing opposition is distinguished by its interest in producing an alternative model of how a non-racist society may be accomplished: it is not merely a negative critique but a statement of faith in the market's ability to *deliver* racial equality. A core claim of this form of analysis is that government-sponsored equity initiatives have deleterious consequences for the victims of racism (Murray, 1984; Steele, 1991). One of the most productive of the scholars aligned to this camp is Thomas Sowell (1981, 1990). Sowell has tried to show that welfare schemes, including affirmative action, encourage dependence and undermine qualities of self-reliance and self-worth. Thus he contrasts 'incentive versus hope' (1990, p. 169). Sowell contends that a free market is a prerequisite for the development and display of social and economic achievement. He explains that within a free market discrimination costs the discriminator money. Thus, for example, 'When apartments remain vacant because minority tenants are turned away, the landlord pays a cost for discrimination. So does the discriminating employer whose jobs remain unfilled longer or can be filled more quickly only at higher pay' (1981, p. 20).

Another conservative critic, Charles Murray (1984), has argued that affirmative action, and, indeed, all social welfare schemes, must be swept away: 'My proposal for dealing with the racial issue in social welfare is to repeal every bit of social legislation and reverse every court decision that in any way requires, recommends or awards differential treatment according to race.' In similar vein, Lewis (1988) has called for the repealing of British anti-racist legislation. In the concluding chapter of *Anti-racism: A Mania Exposed*, he pits the 'race relations industry' against the free markets' ability to create wealth and social mobility among British 'ethnic minorities'.

> Repealing the 1968 [Race Relations Act], then, would not only dispense with most of the general staff of the race relations army but would also dramatically reduce the race relations personnel in many private organisations and firms ... Britain's blacks have a huge potential for their own success and for the contribution they can make to national life. The principal reason why they have so far fallen short of fulfilling it is because they have been over-exposed to the combined forces of the race lobby and the left, making excuses in anticipation of their economic failure before they have even begun to try. They have been targeted within the propaganda of those who for their own purposes want Britain's blacks to regard themselves as underdogs and to believe that the 'system', meaning competitive capitalism, is against them ... [However], precisely because it is colour-blind, the free-market is their friend.
>
> (ibid., pp. 153–156)

Clearly, setting anti-racism in opposition to the free market turns the development of corporate anti-racism and the existence of anti-racist polices in a number of successful capitalist societies around the world into a somewhat embarrassing problem. Both phenomena tend to be ignored by right-wing critics or explained by reference to fashion and muddle-headedness. A less superficial approach is taken by Sowell (1990) in *Preferential Policies: An International Perspective*, a book that, somewhat exceptionally within either the British or North American debate, explores the fact that 'preference policies' may be found all over the globe. Sowell's explanation of 'why they have become so popular and spread so rapidly around the world' (ibid., p. 166) relies on the notion that 'preference policies' offer political elites a 'quick fix' solution to seemingly intractable ethnic conflicts. However, Sowell fails to confront the fact that preference policies have advanced hand in hand with capitalist economies or, indeed, that advanced capitalism relies on national and international state intervention to manage, co-ordinate and sustain its affairs. This absence points to the existence of an irony within this group of commentators' militant advocacy of the free market. For, despite their implicit claims to be in touch with the demands of business, their interpretation of the needs and nature of modern capitalism has a decidedly old-fashioned ring to it. The form of non- or anti-statist capitalism they wish to defend (in which all social outcomes are left to the market) simply no longer exists (if it ever did). Indeed, it appears an unviable and utopian notion when set against the complex, interdependent, nature of contemporary relations between international governance, national governments and capital.

The coherence of the idea that providing socio-economic assistance for a racial group undermines the socio-economic status and prospects of that group must also be questioned. It is pertinent to note that, within the British and North American debates, this argument is focused largely on non-whites. The existence of centuries of social assistance to whites, to the middle class, and to men and other privileged groups tends to be ignored. Once again, it is a view that evidences a rather wishful comprehension of the workings of the free market. The notion that those groups who have 'made it' in today's society (i.e. whites, males, the middle and upper classes) have done so through the mechanism of *open* economic competition bears little historical scrutiny.

THE LEFT VERSUS ANTI-RACISM

It is important to note that most of the left-wing critics I shall be addressing in this section are not merely critical of the liberalism and cultural focus of multiculturalism (a phenomenon identified in Chapters 3 and 4). Although they may share this disposition, they also express a deeper sense of misgiving about what they see as the privileging of issues of race and racism in left politics: anti-racism, they tend to argue, is 'all very well', but it should not be allowed to fragment and distract the left to the detriment of 'the bigger picture'. Thus anti-racism and multiculturalism are aligned with the dilution of class politics and/or with 'the rise of identity politics', 'postmodernism' and other problematic tendencies supposedly characteristic of contemporary capitalism. As this line of attack suggests, one of the defining features of left-wing criticism is its assertion of the mutual dependence of socialism and universalism. Anti-racism is positioned as a conservative subversion of this relationship. Its alignment with social fragmentation and anti-egalitarian relativism requires, however, a very particular and narrow idea of what anti-racism was, is or could be.

For class politics: against fragmentation

Marxist and anarchist communist political analysis of capitalism relies on class as its primordial social category. Class division is seen as the most significant thing that shapes capitalist society. Racial division is regarded as a by-product of this conflict. Allied to this perspective is the notion that racial inequality will inevitably fade as a consequence of class revolution. This position has been articulated by the leaders of many communist states in the twentieth century. The decision not to assert racism as an issue within a communist national project, even by those with direct experience of it, finds an interesting reflection in the support provided by many Afro-Cubans for the 1959 revolution in Cuba. As explained by McGarrity and Cárdenas (1995, p. 95) 'many black revolutionaries rationalised to themselves that, as the goal of the revolutionary process was so valuable, they would overlook persistent racism, trusting that ... racist attitudes would fade away'.

Within capitalist societies, socialist and communist parties and groups have often provided substantial support for anti-racism. However, this support is usually offered on the understanding that the issue of racism is subordinate to that of class struggle. Thus British Marxists have played a key role in organising anti-racist (especially anti-neo-Nazi) campaigns in Britain on the understanding that anti-racism will take its 'proper place' in a 'wider' struggle. As the former Trotskyist Tariq Ali noted, 'Lots of people will come along for Rock Against Racism today and see that it should be Rock Against the Stock Exchange tomorrow' (cited by Gilroy, 1987a, p. 134). As this implies, once anti-racism is seen as setting its own political agenda, and of being uncoupled from the wider struggle, it may be politically re-positioned as a potential enemy of socialist revolution. Tom Hastie (1986), writing 'as a lifelong Socialist' (p. 59) alongside the conservative critics in *Anti-racism: An Assault on Education and Value*, notes:

> As a Socialist I am constantly being astonished how the race industry, which likes to project a 'Red' image, follows a policy of blaming whites *per se* for the problems of our society and makes no reference to the real culprit, the capitalist class, which includes blacks as well as whites.
>
> (ibid., p. 73)

Ironically the main target of Hastie's article is the Institute of Race Relations, which, as the title of its journal – *Race and Class* – suggests, has sought to bring anti-racism and class politics together. Indeed, Hastie seems unaware that writers within the Institute of Race Relations have been severe critics of most varieties of anti-racism, especially those of a confessional, individualistic, nature. As with conservative critics, a strategic misreading of the evidence, and the development of a rather myopic stereotype of anti-racism, is central to Hastie's ability to reject it.

Many left-wing critiques of anti-racism align it with other so-called 'issue-based' forms of politics. Thus, anti-racism, feminism, lesbian and gay movements are all associated as components of a turn away from 'real politics' and towards a post-modern, consumer capitalist-inclined, celebration of difference. Within this perspective, anti-racism is not portrayed as something that needs radicalising but as something inherently limited and limiting. The conflation of anti-racism with identity politics relies on a neglect of those historical aspects of anti-racism that are universalist and/or integrated in class politics. It also relies on the conviction that the left was once united, that it once shared a common universalist agenda. In this way the history of both racial and class politics is misrepresented and foreshortened. Indeed, the former becomes merely another aspect of the 'decline of modernist identity' (Friedman, 1992, p. 361), a decline associated, by Friedman, with the search for 'traditionalist–religious– ethnic' forms of personal meaning. Gitlin (1994) contrasts the 'idea of the Left' which 'relies on the Enlightenment – the belief in the universal human capacity, and need for reason', with a recent 'fragmentation of the idea of the left' with its attendant 'opening of political initiative to minorities, women, gays' (ibid., p. 152). The idea that the 'political initiative' of 'minorities' (by which Gitlin appears to mean people of non-European origin) has only just occurred, that such 'initiative' was not there before, during and after the period when the idea of 'the left' was founded, is a strange one. Yet it has become an almost standard conceit within many radical overviews of postmodern capitalism. Another more worked-through example of this train of thought may be found within the writings of the Marxist geographer, David Harvey. Writing about the lack of political mobilisation in the aftermath of the deaths of black women workers at a chicken processing factory in the USA, he identifies the culprit as 'identity politics' and the 'post-modern critique of universalisms'. In other words,

[the] increasing fragmentation of 'progressive' politics around special issues and the rise of the so-called new social move-ments focusing on gender, race, ethnicity, ecology, multiculturalism, community, and the like. These movements often became a working and practical alternative to class poli-tics of the traditional sort and, in some instances, have exhibited downright hostility to such politics.

(Harvey, 1993, p. 47)

It seems that, for Harvey, as 'race, ethnicity ... multiculturalism' ('and the like') rise, so class falls; where once there was solidarity now there is fragmentation. Any sense that class politics was always racialised in America, that 'race, ethnicity ... multicultur-alism' are far from recent aberrations, is lost, to be replaced by a embattled sense of loss for a mythic time of socialist together-ness.

Anti-racism as moralism

In contrast to the alignment of anti-racism with amoral postmod-ernism one of the other principal challenges to anti-racism asserted most vociferously from the left is the contention that anti-racism displays bourgeois moralism. In this discourse simi-larities are often identified between anti-racism and religious and individualist forms of ideology. For many critics this aspect of anti-racism is an unfortunate tendency rather than an inherent quality. This is the case within the analysis of Macdonald *et al.* (1989), who have isolated what they call 'moral anti-racism' as 'an unmitigated disaster'. Identifying moral anti-racism with what I have termed in Chapter 3 psychological anti-racism, Macdonald *et al.* continue:

> It reinforced the guilt of many well-meaning whites and paral-ysed them when any issue of race arises or has taught others to bury their racism without in any way changing their attitude and has created resentment and anger and stopped free discussion. It encourages the aspiring black middle class to play the 'skin game' and for a few 'liberal anti-racist' whites to collude in it. It has put a few unrepresentative blacks into posi-tions of false power.
>
> (ibid., p. 402)

The apparent overlap between such sentiments and the conserva-tive critique of the 'race relations industry' is somewhat deceptive. For conservative critics publicly funded anti-racist organisations appear to be, almost by definition, unnecessary and/or objectionable. For Macdonald *et al.*, by contrast, moralism is associated with a lack of political engagement, with a retreat from public 'ownership' of anti-racism, a retreat from anti-racism as a project shared among everyone, to a private, internalised process based on emotions of shame and fear.

The most thorough critique of anti-racist moralism has been made by Taguieff in *Les Fins de l'antiracisme* (1995). Taguieff argues that moralism pervades the anti-racist movement in France. It is, he notes, a romantic and sentimental tendency that enables the development of authoritarian and doctrinaire codes of conduct and behaviour. Moralistic anti-racism is portrayed by Taguieff as structured upon crypto-theological categories; racism being seen as evil, as sin, and as disease, and anti-racists as the forces of light and goodness. 'Absolute evil is naturalised in anti-racist discourse ... the eternal return of the tendency towards racism plays the role of original sin in the pseudo-theology of anti-racism' (ibid., p. 457).

Commenting on the *'reductio ad Hitlerum'* that he claims characterises much anti-racist thinking (i.e. the idea that racism leads to Nazism and/or that Nazism was the most authentic expression of racism, the baseline against which all racisms must be judged), Taguieff goes on to suggest that

> The idea of absolute corruption, irreversible and complete defilement, returns in anti-racist discourse against the racist enemy from whom it has been borrowed. Thus it appears as a polemical theme common to both racism and anti-racism. This has real consequences for anti-racist action: if racists are unreformable, irredeemable, stained by their sins, then only one strategy becomes available, to dispel them, to 'neutralise' them, in a word, segregation.
>
> (ibid., p. 464)

Taguieff's portrait of anti-racism certainly invites indignation. If anti-racism is, indeed, so crude, so brutal and moralistic then it demands rebuke. But although Taguieff may be said to have offered a useful portrait of an element within anti-racism, the narrowness of his examples and geographical and historical focus make his a very partial vision. Indeed, Taguieff's illustrations of anti-racist activity are suspiciously sketchy and abstract.

Moreover, moralism is a more slippery term of abuse than Taguieff implies. After all, without a moral impetus why should we support anti-racism at all, other than for purely managerial reasons of control? As we have seen in the discussion of essentialism, the deployment of simplistic categories, such as black, white, good, bad, is not simply a matter of intellectual choice; such labels may be problematic but it is difficult to envisage a form of effective politics, a politics that can engage and challenge racism, that entirely dispenses with them. Moralism may be a problem within anti-racism, but it is a problem that needs to be acknowledged, to be lived with, rather than solved or banished.

CONCLUSION

Anti-racism has been reviled, dismissed and critiqued by so many people it can sometimes appear as if everybody is approaching it from a critical angle. Indeed, as if 'it' itself is a mere chimera, and once one had pushed aside all the critics one would find nothing, except perhaps a hall of distorting mirrors. This sensation arises because many of the critics drawn on above rely on a narrow – historically, geographically and politically – interpretation of what anti-racism means. They have tended to construct stereotypes of anti-racism based on limited examples, stereotypes which they employ for strategic political purposes. Indeed, it can seem that the grandness of the critique is proportional to the narrowness of its grasp: anti-racism is crisply summarised and dispatched as 'extremist' or 'fractional' with little regard to its subtleties or variations. If these critics were somewhat more reflexive about the limitations of their interventions, if they were more willing to specify that they are addressing a particular variety of anti-racism at a particular time, and indicate which varieties they do support and why (after all, all these critics claim not to be racist), their pronouncements might, just might, be judged as contributions to anti-racist debate. As it is, they are a necessary component of anti-racism's story largely because of their power to shape the way anti-racism is (mis)understood and (mis)represented.

6

CONCLUSION

The twentieth century has been witness to many examples of racial hatred and dominance, of ethnic exclusion and marginalisation, of wars fought, conquests made and genocides undertaken, in the name of 'blood' and 'kin'. Whether the twenty-first century endures a similar fate depends on those forces that oppose the development and dissemination of racist attitudes and practices. It depends, in other words, on anti-racism. The prospects of success are not helped by the fact that over recent years a certain complacency has grown up around matters of race and racism. 'No one believes in biological hierarchy any more' we are told: anti-racism is irrelevant, an anachronism. Indeed, as Chapter 5 indicated, anti-racism appears to annoy many commentators; they stereotype it, construct it as risible, then mock their own creation. And so one of the twentieth century's most complex and diverse forces of resistance to oppression and social terror is alienated from ordinary people, cut off from social ownership: a resource for enabling humane societies and humane solutions to future conflict is deprived of support and serious debate. It is necessary to explain, then, that anti-racism has rarely simply been about opposition to biological racism. It certainly contains that tradition (and it is worth noting that it is a tradition that, despite being an 'anachronism' among the scientific and intellectual community, finds itself in many countries engaged in combating *rising* levels of neo-Nazi racism). But anti-racism has also engaged many other forms of discriminatory discourse, such as the naturalisation of ethnic difference, the practice of cultural and religious exclusion, and the formation of negative and homogenising attitudes towards outcast and 'othered' groups.

Contemporary discussions of anti-racism are often marked by their parochialism. Various 'national traditions' and 'national debates' have arisen around the world characterised by insular, and often nationalistic, forms of knowledge and practice. The claim to 'tolerance' is selfishly guarded by states and other institutions concerned to legitimise themselves by reference to their social egalitarianism. Ironically, this situation accentuates the impact of the one country whose race equity practices do have a global audience, the USA. In the mid to late twentieth century American racial categories and the American history of race were adopted and adapted across the world. This dominance has ensured that many 'national debates' on anti-racism are structured around the conceit of a dialogue between 'our approach' and what goes on in the USA. The rise of 'global culture' suggests that this situation is likely to become even more common. It also indicates that those traditions of resistance against racial and ethnic discrimination that are unable or unwilling to situate themselves in relation to this master narrative will find themselves increasingly marginal and overlooked. In Chapter 2 I mentioned the way that contemporary activists in Peru associate anti-racism with something that has 'come in' from the West, as something separate from the history of Peruvian opposition to racism and ethnic discrimination. It is a situation that displaces this latter history to the realm of 'local interest', a research concern for 'regional' and 'ethnic specialists'. A corollary of this process is that anti-racism can appear irrelevant within situations that cannot be comprehended within its dominant rhetorical repertoire of 'white racism' and 'non-white struggle'. Given the fact that ethnicity is so often deployed as a euphemism for what are, in fact, naturalised and naturalising forms of discrimination and hatred, this kind of restriction is both misleading and unjustifiable. Moreover, as argued in Chapter 4, the notion that anti-racism is not pertinent to 'ethnic conflict' is extraordinarily wasteful of a highly developed and practical resource for understanding, engaging and resolving such situations. In part, the difficulty of accommodating anti-racism to ethnicity lies in the very invisibility of the essentialist and naturalising currents that animate the latter. Anti-racism is, after all, widely associated with not merely wanting to abolish racism but with placing race itself under scrutiny, of disturbing the foundations upon which racial knowledge and experience are built. The core categories of 'ethnic conflict' are rarely allowed to be subjected to a comparable scrutiny. However reified their usage, constructs of the Chinese, the Jews, the Irish and so on are nearly always offered as terms, as experiences, that must be 'respected'. Yet there is no more reason to respect the lie that such groups are natural formations with immutable attributes and clear boundaries, than there is to respect the fantasy of race. The engagement of anti-racism with ethnicity contains the potential to extend and deepen the critique of the naturalisation of group difference into new and diverse areas.

Any such expansion of the terrain of anti-racism would need, however, to be mindful of the fact that anti-racism has been and remains marked by contradiction and the interaction of traditions. The notion of pure resistance is a myth. Anti-racism is more realistically portrayed as a form of struggle within and against the social norms and forces that surround and enable it (including racism, including capitalism). Thus, for example, as Chapter 1 indicated, universalism and relativism contain resources for both racism and anti-racism. Similar complicity and tension may be found in many of the other antecedents and contemporary forms of anti-racism. Moreover, these traditions are interconnected: the histories of Western and non-Western anti-racisms are mingled; each drawing on the other to the point where the term 'Western' becomes intelligible only as a geographical and racial conceit, albeit a highly influential one.

Anti-racism has been one of the central liberatory currents of the twentieth century. It may be located in the struggle against European colonialism, and in the attempt to form multiracial, multicultural, international and national forms of governance. It can be seen at work in the development of forms of education and training that facilitate tolerant and cosmopolitan attitudes, as well as within everyday culture. If we are to be able to build on such work, and identify and oppose racism in the future, the development of and ideologies behind these forms of resistance need to be understood and made the subject of debate. I would also argue that such a project needs to be unsentimental and alert to the contradictions of its subject matter. The history of anti-racism is not simply a story of heroic struggle. Very often it is not the history of heroes at all, but something more mundane, more tarnished, more recognisably a part of all our lives.

BIBLIOGRAPHY

Abdul-Raheem, T. (ed.) (1996) *Pan Africanism: Politics, Economy and Social Change in the Twenty-first Century*, London: Pluto Press.

Adam, H. (1992) 'Ethnicity, nationalism and the state', in K. Moodley (ed.) *Beyond Multicultural Education: International Perspectives*, Calgary: Detselig Enterprise, pp. 14–22.

Allen, T. (1994) *The Invention of the White Race: Volume One: Racial Oppression and Social Control*, London: Verso.

Amos, V. and Parmar, P. (1984) 'Challenging imperialist feminism', *Feminist Review* 17, pp. 3–19.

Andrews, G. (1994) 'Black political protest in São Paulo, 1888–1988', in J. Domínguez (ed.) *Race and Ethnicity in Latin America*, New York: Garland Publishing, pp. 303–328.

Anthias, F. and Yuval-Davis, N. (1992) *Racialized Boundaries: Race, Nation, Gender, Colour and Class and the Anti-racist Struggle*, London: Routledge.

Appiah, A. (1986) 'The uncompleted argument: Du Bois and the illusion of race', in H. Gates Jr. (ed.) *'Race', Writing and Difference*, Chicago: University of Chicago Press, pp. 21–37.

Aptheker, H. (1993) *Anti-racism in U.S. History: The First Two Hundred Years*, Westport, Conn: Praeger.

Bagley, C. (1989) 'Education for all: a Canadian dimension', in G. Verma (ed.) *Education for All: A Landmark in Pluralism*, Lewes: Falmer Press, pp. 98–117.

Baker, H. (1986) 'Caliban's triple play', *Critical Inquiry* 13, 1, pp. 182–196.

Baker, K. (1987) Speech to the Annual Conservative Conference, Blackpool, 7 October.

Balibar, E. and Wallerstein, I. (1991) *Race, Nation, Class: Ambiguous Identities*, London: Verso.

Ball, W. and Solomos, J. (eds) (1990) *Race and Local Politics*, London: Macmillan.

Banton, M. (1994a) 'The Twelfth Report of the United Kingdom under the International Convention on the Elimination of all Forms of Racial Discrimination', *New Community* 20, 3, pp. 488–496.

—— (1994b) 'The Twelfth Report of Germany under the International Convention on the Elimination of all Forms of Racial Discrimination', *New Community* 20, 3, pp. 496–501.

—— (1998) 'European policy report', *Journal of Ethnic and Migration Studies* 24, 1, pp. 209–216.

Barkan, E. (1992) *The Retreat of Scientific Racism: Changing Concepts of Race in Britain and the United States Between the World Wars*, Cambridge: Cambridge University Press.

Bates, S. (1995) 'Fury as Howard blocks race law', *The Guardian*, 24 November.

Bell, B., Grosholz, E. and Stewart, J. (eds) (1996) *W.E.B. Du Bois on Race and Culture*, New York: Routledge.

Bhabha, H. (1990) 'Interview with Homi Bhabha: The Third Space', in J. Rutherford (ed.) *Identity: Community, Culture and Difference*, London: Lawrence and Wishart, pp. 207–221.

Biggs-Davison, J. (1972) *Africa: Hope Deferred*, London: Johnson.

Bollinger, W. and Lund, D. (1994) 'Minority oppression: towards analyses that clarify and strategies that liberate', in J. Domínguez (ed.) *Race and Ethnicity in Latin America*, New York: Garland Publishing, pp. 218–244.

Bonnett, A. (1992) 'Anti-racism in "white" areas: the example of Tyneside', *Antipode* 24, 1, pp. 1–15.

—— (1993a) *Radicalism, Anti-racism and Representation*, London: Routledge.

—— (1993b) 'Contours of crisis: anti-racism and reflexivity', in P. Jackson and J. Penrose (eds) *Constructions of Race, Place and Nation*, London: UCL Press, pp. 163–180.

—— (1997) 'Constructions of whiteness in European and American anti-racism' , in P. Werbner and T. Modood (eds) *Debating Cultural Hybridity: Multi-Cultural Identities and the Politics of Anti-racism*, London: Zed Press, pp. 173–192.

—— (1998) 'How the British working class became white: the symbolic (re)formation of racialized capitalism', *Journal of Historical Sociology* 11, 3, pp. 316–340.

—— (1999) *White Identities: Historical and International Perspectives*, Harlow: Prentice Hall.

Bonnett, A. and Carrington, B. (1996) 'Constructions of anti-racist education in Britain and Canada' , *Comparative Education* 32, 3, pp. 271–288.

Bourne, J. (1983) 'Towards an anti-racist feminism', *Race and Class* 25, 1, pp. 1–22.

Brah, A. (1996) *Cartographies of Diaspora: Contesting Identities*, London: Routledge.

Brandt, G. (1986) *The Realization of Anti-racist Teaching*, Lewes: The Falmer Press.

Bulhan, H. (1985) *Frantz Fanon and the Psychology of Oppression*, New York: Plenum Books.

Bullivant, B. (1981) *The Pluralist Dilemma in Education*, Sydney: Allen and Unwin.

Carby, H. (1982) 'White woman listen: black feminism and the boundaries of sisterhood', in Centre for Contemporary Cultural Studies (ed.) *The Empire Strikes Back: Race and Racism in 80s Britain*, London: Hutchinson.

—— (1998) *Race Men*, Cambridge, MA: Harvard University Press.

Carrington, B. and Bonnett, A. (1997) 'The other Canadian "mosaic" – "race" equity education in Ontario and British Columbia', *Comparative Education* 33, 3, pp. 411–431.

Castles, S. and Kosack, G. (1972) 'The function of labour immigration in Western European capitalism', *New Left Review* 73, pp. 3–21.

Chaudhuri, N. and Strobel, M. (eds) (1992) *Western Women and Imperialism: Complicity and Resistance*, Bloomington: Indiana University Press.

Chowdhury, A. and Islam, I. (1996) 'The institutional and political framework of growth in an ethnically diverse society: the case of Malaysia', *Canadian Journal of Development Studies* 17, 3, pp. 487–512.

Clark, A. (1998) 'Race, "culture" and mestizaje: the statistical construction of the Ecuadorian nation, 1930–1950', *Journal of Historical Sociology* 11, 2, pp. 185–211.

Clark, G. and Subhan, N. (undated) 'Some definitions', in K. Ebbutt and B. Pearce (eds) *Racism and Schools: Contributions to a Discussion*, London: Communist Party of Great Britain.

Clarke, J. (1997) *Oriental Enlightenment: The Encounter Between Asian and Western Thought*, London: Routledge.

Combahee River Collective (1986) *The Combahee River Collective Statement: Black Feminist Organizing in the Seventies and Eighties*, New York: Women of Color Press.

Comber, L. (1988) *13 May 1969: A Historical Survey of Sino-Malay Relations*, Singapore: Graham Brash (Pte) Ltd.

Comte, A. (1851–1854) *Système de politique positive*, 4 volumes, Paris: L. Mathias.

Costa-Lascoux, J. (1994) 'French legislation against racism and discrimination', *New Community* 20, 3, pp. 371–379.

Covin, D. (1990) 'Afrocentricity in *O Movimento Negro Unificado*', *Journal of Black Studies* 21, 2, pp. 126–144.

Cox, O. (1970) *Caste, Class and Race*, New York: Monthly Review Press.

Cross, M. (1997) 'The new European Monitoring Centre' http://www.ercomer.org/merger/vol...eNewEuropeanMonitoringCentre.html

Cruz, J. (1996) 'From farce to tragedy: reflections on the reification of race at century's end', in A. Gordon and C. Newfield (eds) *Mapping Multiculturalism*, Minneapolis: University of Minnesota Press, pp. 19–39.

Cunha, O. (1998) 'Black movements and the "politics of identity" in Brazil', in S. Alverez, E. Dagnino and A. Escobar (eds) *Cultures of Politics, Politics of Cultures: Re-visioning Latin American Social Movements*, Boulder, Col: Westview Press, pp. 220–251.

Dikötter, F. (1992) *The Discourse of Race in Modern China*, Stanford, CA: Stanford University Press.

Dominguez, V. (1994) 'A taste for "the Other": intellectual complicity in racializing practices', *Current Anthropology* 35, 4, pp. 333–338.

D'Souza, D. (1991) *Illiberal Education: The Politics of Race and Sex on Campus*, New York: Free Press.

—— (1995) *The End of Racism: Principles for a Multiracial Society*, New York: Free Press.

Du Bois, W. (1965) *The World and Africa: An Inquiry into the Part which Africa Has Played in World History*, New York: International Publishers.

—— (1968) *Dusk at Dawn: An Essay Toward an Autobiography of a Race Concept*, New York: Schocken Books.

—— (1970) *W. E. B. Du Bois Speaks: Speeches and Addresses, 1899–1963*, volume 1, New York: Pathfinder Press.

—— (1985) *Against Racism: Unpublished Essays, Papers, Addresses, 1887–1961*, Amherst, MA: University of Massachusetts Press.

—— (1989) *The Souls of Black Folk*, New York: Penguin.

—— (1995) *Black Reconstruction in America: 1860–1880*, New York: Touchstone.

Dyer, C. (1998) 'Race law "does not apply" to Muslims', *The Guardian*, 28 October.

Edwards, J. (1992) 'Multicultural education in a contemporary context', *Canadian Ethnic Studies* 24, pp. 23–34.

—— (1995) *When Race Counts: The Morality of Racial Preference in Britain and America*, London: Routledge.

Eze, E. (ed.) (1997) *Race and the Enlightenment: A Reader*, Oxford: Blackwell.

Fanon, F. (1967) *The Wretched of the Earth*, Harmondsworth: Penguin.

—— (1986) *Black Skin, White Masks*, London: Pluto Press.

Frankenberg, R. (1993) *White Women, Race Matters: The Social Construction of Whiteness*, Minneapolis, MN: University of Minnesota Press.

Fraser, N. (1998) 'From redistribution to recognition? Dilemmas of justice in a "post-socialist" age', in C. Willett (ed.) *Theorizing Multiculturalism: A Guide to the Current Debate*, Oxford: Blackwell, pp. 19–49.

Fredrickson, G. (1988) *The Arrogance of Race: Historical Perspectives on Slavery, Racism, and Social Inequality*, Middletown, CT: Wesleyan University Press.

Friedman, J. (1992) 'Narcissism, roots and postmodernity: the constitution of selfhood in the global crisis', in S. Lash and J. Friedman (eds) *Modernity and Identity*, Oxford: Blackwell, pp. 331–366.

Fryer, P. (1984) *Staying Power: The History of Black People in Britain*, London: Pluto Press.

Fuijimori, A. (1995) 'A momentous decision', in O. Starn, I. Degregori and R. Kirk (eds) *The Peru Reader: History, Culture, Politics*, Durham, NC: Duke University Press.

Füredi, F. (1998) *The Silent War: Imperialism and the Changing Perception of Race*, London: Pluto Press.

Fuss, D. (1989) *Essentially Speaking: Feminism, Nature and Difference*, New York: Routledge.

Gabriel, J. (1994) *Racism, Culture, Markets*, London: Routledge.

—— (1998) *Whitewash: Racialized Politics and the Media*, London: Routledge.

Gaines, S. Jr. (1996) 'Perspectives of Du Bois and Fanon on the psychology of oppression', in L. Gordon, T. Sharpley-Whiting and R. White (eds) *Fanon: A Critical Reader*, Oxford: Blackwell, pp. 24–34.

Garvey, J. and Ignatiev, N. (1997) 'Toward a new abolitionism: A *Race Traitor* manifesto', in M. Hill (ed.) *Whiteness: A Critical Reader*, New York: New York University Press, pp. 346–350.

Gates, H. Jr. (1985) 'Writing "race" and the difference it makes', *Critical Inquiry* 12, 1, pp. 1–20.

Genovese, E. (1976) *Roll, Jordan, Roll: The World the Slaves Made*, New York: Vintage Books.

Gilroy, P. (1987a) *There Ain't No Black in the Union Jack: The Cultural Politics of Race and Nation*, London: Macmillan.

—— (1987b) *Problems in Anti-racist Strategy*, London: Runnymede Trust.

—— (1990) 'The end of anti-racism', *New Community* 17, pp. 71–84.

—— (1993) *The Black Atlantic: Modernity and Double Consciousness*, London: Verso.

Gitlin, T. (1994) 'From universality to difference: notes on the fragmentation of the idea of the left', in C. Calhoun (ed.) *Social Theory and the Politics of Identity*, Oxford: Blackwell, pp. 150–174.

Goldberg, D. (ed.) (1994) *Multiculturalism: A Critical Reader*, Oxford: Blackwell.

—— (1996) 'In/visibility and super/vision: Fanon on race, veils, and discourses of resistance', in L. Gordon, T. Sharpley-Whiting and R. White (eds) *Fanon: A Critical Reader*, Oxford: Blackwell, pp. 179–202.

Goldsmith, O. (1934) *The Citizen of the World: or Letters from a Chinese Philosopher Residing in London to His Friend in the East*, London: J. M. Dent.

Gonález, L. (1985) 'The Unified Black Movement: a new stage in black political mobilization', in P-M. Fontaine (ed.) *Race, Class and Power in Brazil*, Los Angeles: Center for Afro-American Studies, University of California, pp. 120–134.

Gordon, P. (1990) 'A dirty war: the New Right and Local Authority anti-racism', in W. Ball and J. Solomos (eds) *Race and Local Politics*, London: Macmillan.

Gordon, P. and Klug, F. (1986) *New Right, New Racism*, London: Searchlight Publications.

Government of Malaysia (1971) *Second Malaysia Plan, 1971–75*, Kuala Lumpur: Government Printer.

Green, A. (1982) 'In defence of anti-racist teaching: a reply to recent critiques of multicultural education', *Multiracial Education* 10, 2, pp. 19–35.

Grimshaw, J. (1986) *Philosophy and Feminist Thinking*, Minneapolis: University of Minnesota Press.

Grugeon, E. and Wood, P. (1990) *Educating All: Multicultural Perspectives in the Primary School*, London: Routledge.

Guimarães, A. (1995) 'Racism and anti-racism in Brazil: a postmodern perspective', in B. Bowser (ed.) *Racism and Anti-racism in World Perspective*, Thousand Oaks, CA: Sage, pp. 208–226.

Gurnah, A. (1984) 'The Politics of Racism Awareness Training', *Critical Social Policy* 11, 6–20.

Hanchard, M. (1994) *Orpheus and Power: The Movimento Negro of Rio de Janeiro and São Paulo, Brazil, 1945–1988*, Princeton, NJ: Princeton University Press.

Harvey, D. (1993) 'Class relations, social justice and the politics of difference', in M. Keith and S. Pile (eds) *Place and the Politics of Identity*, London: Routledge, pp. 41–66.

Hastie, T. (1986) 'History, race and propaganda', in F. Palmer (ed.) *Anti-racism: An Assault on Education and Value*, London: The Sherwood Press, pp. 61–73.

Hatcher, R. (1983) 'The politics of anti-racist education', *Multiracial Education* 12, 1, pp. 3–21.

Hebdige, D. (1979) *Subculture: The Meaning of Style*, London: Methuen.

Hiro, D. (1971) *Black British, White British*, London: Eyre and Spottiswoode.

Hobsbawm, E. (1992) *Nations and Nationalism Since 1780: Programme, Myth, Reality*, second edition, Cambridge: Cambridge University Press.

Hodson, H. (1950) 'Race relations in the Commonwealth', *International Affairs* 26, pp. 303–315.

Honeyford, R. (1986) 'Anti-racist rhetoric', in F. Palmer (ed.) *Anti-racism: An Assault on Education and Value*, London: The Sherwood Press, pp. 43–60.

hooks, b. (1984) *Feminist Theory: From Margin to Centre*, Boston: South End Press.

Hopenhayn, M. (1993) 'Postmodernism and neoliberalism in Latin America', *Boundary* 2 20, 3, pp. 93–109.

Human Rights Library (1998) *The African Commission on Human Rights and Peoples' Rights Examination of State Reports*, 9th Session, March 1991, Rwanda http://www.umn.edu/humanrts/achpr/sess9-Rwanda.htm

Huxley, J., Haddon, A. and Carr-Saunders, A. (1939) *We Europeans: A Survey of 'Racial' Problems*, Harmondsworth: Penguin Books.

i-D (1994) 124, January.

Ignatiev, N. (1995) *How the Irish Became White*, New York: Routledge.

—— (1997) discussion on *The Colin Bell Show*, BBC Radio Scotland, 10 December.

Inner London Education Authority (1983) *Race, Sex and Class: 2. Multiethnic Education in Schools*, London: Inner London Education Authority.

James, C.L.R. (1994) *The Black Jacobins: Toussaint L'Ouverture and the San Domingo Revolution*, London: Allison and Busby.

James, D. (1993) *Negrophobia: An Urban Parable: A Novel*, New York: St Martin's Press.

Jeffcoate, R. (1979) *Positive Image: Towards a Multiracial Curriculum*, London: Writers and Readers Publishing Cooperative.

Jesudason, J. (1989) *Ethnicity and the Economy: The State, Chinese Business and Multinationals in Malaysia*, Singapore: Oxford University Press.

Jones, S. (1989) *Black Culture, White Youth: The Reggae Tradition from JA to UK*, London: Macmillan.

Joyce, J. (1987) 'The Black Canon: reconstructing black American literary criticism', *New Literary History* 18, 2, pp. 335–344.

Kahlenberg, R. (1995) 'Class, not race', *New Republic* 3 April.

Katz, J. (1978) *White Awareness: Handbook for Anti-racism Training*, Norman, OK: University of Oklahoma Press.

Knight, A. (1990) 'Racism, revolution, and indigenismo: Mexico, 1910–1940', in R. Graham (ed.) *The Idea of Race in Latin America, 1870–1940*, Austin, TX: University of Texas Press, pp.71–114.

Knowles, C. and Mercer, S. (1992) 'Feminism and antiracism: an exploration of the political possibilities', in J. Donald and A. Rattansi (eds) *'Race', Culture and Difference*, London: Sage, pp. 104–148.

Laurie, N. and Bonnett, A. (forthcoming) 'Adjusting to equity: the contradictions of neo-liberalism and the search for racial equality in Peru' *Antipode*.

Lecky, W. (1869) *History of European Morals from Augustus to Charlemagne*, London: Longmans, Green and Company.

Leman, J. (1996) 'Europe's Consultative Commission on Racism and Xenophobia and the slow progress towards a European Antiracism Observatory', *Loyola of Los Angeles International and Comparative Law Journal* 18, 3, pp. 603–612.

Levine, J. (1994) 'The heart of whiteness: dismantling the master's house', *Voice Literary Supplement* 128, pp. 11–16.

Levine, L. (1977) *Black Culture and Black Consciousness: Afro-American Folk Thought from Slavery to Freedom*, New York: Oxford University Press.

Lewis, B. (1971) *Race and Color in Islam*, New York: Harper and Row.

Lewis, Rupert (1987) 'Garvey's forerunners: Love and Bedward', *Race and Class* 28, 3, pp. 29–40.

Lewis, Russell (1988) *Anti-racism: A Mania Exposed*, London: Quartet Books.

Lewis, S. (1992) letter to Premier Bob Rae (unpublished).

Lienhard, M. (1997) 'Of mestizajes, heterogeneities, hybridisms and other chimeras: on the macroprocesses of cultural interaction in Latin America', *Journal of Latin American Cultural Studies* 6, 2, pp. 183–200.

Lloyd, C. (1991) 'Concepts, models and anti-racist strategies in Britain and France', *New Community* 18, 1, pp. 63–73.

—— (1993a) 'International comparisons in the field of ethnic relations', paper presented to the conference on Racism, Ethnicity and Politics, Loughborough, Loughborough University.

—— (1993b) 'Research and policy issues in a European perspective', in J. Wench and J. Solomos (eds) *Racism and Migration in Western Europe*, Oxford: Berg, pp. 251–263.

—— (1994) 'Universalism and difference: the crisis of anti-racism in the UK and France', in A. Rattansi and S. Westwood (eds) *Racism, Modernity and Identity*, Oxford: Polity, pp. 222–244.

—— (1998) *Discourses of Antiracism in France*, Aldershot: Ashgate.

Logan, R. (ed.) (1971) *W.E.B. Du Bois: A Profile*, New York: Hill and Wang.

London Edinburgh Weekend Return Group (1980) *In and Against the State*, London: Pluto Press.

McCulloch, J. (1983) *Black Soul, White Artifact: Fanon's Clinical Psychology and Social Theory*, Cambridge: Cambridge University Press.

Macdonald, I. *et al.* (1989) *Murder in the Playground: The Report of the*

Macdonald Inquiry into Racism and Racial Violence in Manchester Schools, London: Longsight Press.

MacEwen, M. (1995) *Tackling Racism in Europe: An Examination of Anti-discrimination Law in Practice*, Oxford: Berg.

McGarrity, G. and Cárdenas, O. (1995) 'Cuba', in Minority Rights Group (eds) *No Longer Invisible: Afro-Latin Americans Today*, London: Minority Rights Publications, pp. 77–108.

Macpherson, W. (1999) *The Stephen Lawrence Inquiry: Report of an Inquiry by Sir William Macpherson of Cluny*, London: HMSO.

Mahathir, M. (1976) speech by Y.A.B. Dr Mahathir Mohammad, Deputy Prime Minister/Education Minister, delivered at Federation of Malaysian Manufactures Seminar on the Third Malaysian Plan, Kuala Lumpur, 26 August.

Majeed, J. (1997) 'Race and pan-Islam in Iqbal's thought', in P. Robb (ed.) *The Concept of Race in South Asia*, Delhi: Oxford University Press, pp. 304–326.

Malik, K. (1996) *The Meaning of Race: Race, History and Culture in Western Society*, Basingstoke: Macmillan.

Mallon, F. (1996) 'Constructing mestizaje in Latin America: authenticity, marginality, and gender in the claiming of ethnic identities', *Journal of Latin Amercan Anthropology* 2, 1, pp. 170–181.

Marable, M. (1996) 'The pan-Africanism of W.E.B. du Bois', in B. Bell, E. Grosholz and J. Stewart (eds) *W.E.B. Du Bois on Race and Culture: Philosophy, Politics and Poetics*, New York: Routledge, pp. 193–218.

Marat, J-P. (1971) *Polish Letters*, New York: Benjamin Blom.

Marks, J. (1986) ' "Anti-racism" – revolution not education', in F. Palmer (ed.) *Anti-racism: An Assault on Education and Value*, London: The Sherwood Press, pp. 32–42.

Martin, T. (1983) *The Pan-African Connection: From Slavery to Garvey and Beyond*, Dover, MA: Majority Press.

Marx, K. (1859) 'Another civilization war', *New York Daily Tribune*, 10 October.

—— (1969) *Karl Marx on Colonialism and Modernization*, New York: Anchor Books.

—— (1974) *The First International and After*, Harmondsworth: Penguin.

—— (1992) *Surveys from Exile: Political Writings*, volume 2, Harmondsworth: Penguin.

May, S. (ed.) (1998) *Critical Multiculturalism: Rethinking Multicultural and Anti-racist Education*, Lewes: Falmer Press.

Memmi, A. (1990) *The Colonizer and the Colonized*, London: Earthscan Books.

Mendoza, Z. (1998) 'Defining folklore: mestizo and indigenous identities on the move', *Bulletin of Latin American Research* 17, 2, pp. 165–184.

Merson, A. (1985) *Communist Resistance in Nazi Germany*, London: Lawrence and Wishart.

Miles, R. (1982) *Racism and Migrant Labour: A Critical Text*, London: Routledge and Kegan Paul.

—— (1989) *Racism*, London: Routledge.

Modood, T. (1988) '"Black", racial equality and Asian identity', *New Community* 14, 3, pp. 397–404.

—— (1990a) 'Catching up with Jesse Jackson: being oppressed and being somebody', *New Community* 17, 1, pp. 85–96.

—— (1990b) 'British Asian Muslims and the Rushdie affair', *Political Quarterly* 61(2), pp. 143–160.

—— (1992) *Not Easy Being British: Colour, Culture and Citizenship*, Stoke-on-Trent: Trentham Books/Runnymede Trust.

—— (1993) 'Muslim views on religious identity and racial equality', *New Community* 19, 3, pp. 513–519.

—— (1994) 'Political blackness and British Asians', *Sociology* 28, 4, pp. 859–876.

—— (1996) 'The changing context of "race" in Britain', *Patterns of Prejudice* 30, 1, pp. 3–12.

Montague, A. (1951) *Statement on Race*, New York: Henry Schuman.

Montaigne, M. (1993) *The Complete Essays*, Harmondsworth: Penguin.

Montesquieu (1973) *Persian Letters*, Harmondsworth: Penguin.

—— (1989) *The Spirit of the Laws*, Cambridge: Cambridge University Press.

Moodley, K. (1992) 'Ethnicity, power, politics and minority education', in K. Moodley (ed.) *Beyond Multicultural Education: International Perspectives*, Calgary: Detselig Enterprises, pp.79–94.

Mörner, M. (1967) *Race Mixture in the History of Latin America*, Boston: Little, Brown and Company.

Mullard, C. (1985) 'Multiracial education in Britain: from assimilation to cultural pluralism', in M. Arnot (ed.) *Race and Gender: Equal Opportunities Policies in Education*, Oxford: Pergamon Press.

Murray, C. (1984) *Losing Ground: American Social Policy, 1950–1980*, New York: Basic Books

Murray, N. (1986) 'Anti-racists and other demons: the press and ideology in Thatcher's Britain', *Race and Class* 27, 3, pp. 1–19.

Muslim Parliament of Great Britain (1992) *Race Relations and Muslims in Great Britain: A Discussion Paper*, London: The Muslim Parliament.

Naoko, S. (1989) 'The Japanese attempt to secure racial equality in 1919', *Japan Forum*, April, pp. 94–95.

Nicosia, F. and Stokes, L. (eds) (1990) *Germans Against Nazism: Essays in Honour of Peter Hoffmann*, New York: Berg.

Offe, C. (1984) *Contradictions of the Welfare State*, London: Hutchinson.

—— (1985) *Disorganized Capitalism*, Cambridge: Polity Press.

O'Keefe, D. (1986) 'Preference and prejudice: the mythology of British racism', in F. Palmer (ed.) *Anti-racism: An Assault on Education and Value*, London: The Sherwood Press, pp. 185–196.

Organisation of African Unity (1998) 'Welcome to the OAU', http://www.rapide-pana.com/demo/oua/rapid3.htlm

Palmer, F. (ed.) (1986) *Anti-racism: An Assault on Education and Value*, London: The Sherwood Press.

Peabody, S. (1996) *'There are no Slaves in France': The Political Culture of Race and Slavery in the Ancien Régime*, New York: Oxford University Press.

Pieterse, J. (1995) 'Globalization as hybridisation', in M. Featherstone, M. Lash and R. Robertson (eds) *Global Modernities*, London: Sage, pp. 45–68.

Polanco, H. (1997) *Indigenous Peoples in Latin America: The Quest for Self-determination*, Boulder, CO: Westview Press.

Powell, E. (1969) *Freedom and Reality*, Kingswood: Elliot Right Way Books.

Pratt, M. (1992) *Imperial Eyes: Travel Writing and Transculturation*, London: Routledge.

Race Traitor (1994) 3.

Rattansi, A. (1992) 'Changing the subject? Racism, culture and education', in A. Rattansi and D. Reeder (eds) *Rethinking Radical Education: Essays in Honour of Brian Simon*, London: Lawrence and Wishart, pp. 52–95.

—— (1994) '"Western" racisms, ethnicities and identities in a "postmodern" frame', in A. Rattansi and S. Westwood (eds) *Racism, Modernity and Identity on the Western Front*, Oxford: Polity Press, pp. 15–86.

Reed, A. Jr. (1997) *W.E.B. Du Bois and American Political Thought: Fabianism and the Color Line*, New York: Oxford University Press.

Roediger, D. (1992) *The Wages of Whiteness: Race and the Making of the American Working Class*, London: Verso.

—— (1994) *Towards the Abolition of Whiteness: Essays on Race, Politics, and Working Class History*, London: Verso.

—— (forthcoming) '"Guineas", "wiggers" and the dramas of racialized culture', *American Literary History*.

Rose, A. (1961) *The Roots of Prejudice*, Paris: UNESCO.

Rosen, J. (1994) 'Is affirmative action doomed?', *New Republic*, 17 October.

Rosenhaft, E. (1993) *Beating the Fascists? The German Communists and Political Violence, 1929–1933*, Cambridge: Cambridge University Press.

Rotaeche, C. (1998) 'Racial discrimination and the European Convention on Human Rights', *Journal of Ethnic and Migration Studies* 24, 1, pp. 177–188.

Rousseau, J-J. (1984) *A Discourse on Inequality*, Harmondsworth: Penguin.

Rubio, P. (1993) 'The "exceptional white" in popular culture', *Race Traitor* 2, pp. 68–80.

Safran, W. (1984) 'The French left and ethnic pluralism', *Ethnic and Racial Studies* 7, 4, pp. 447–461.

Sakamoto, R. (1996) 'Japan, hybridity and the creation of colonialist discourse', *Theory, Culture and Society* 13, 3, pp. 113–128.

Salim, S. (1996) 'The OAU and the future', in T. Abdul-Raheem (ed.) *Pan Africanism: Politics, Economy and Social Change in the Twenty-first Century*, London: Pluto Press, pp. 229–236.

Sartre, J-P. (1967) 'Preface', in F. Fanon, *The Wretched of the Earth*, Harmondsworth: Penguin, pp. 7–26.

Schor, N. (1994) 'Introduction', in N. Schor and E. Weed (eds) *The Essential Difference*, Bloomington: Indiana University Press, pp. vii–xix.

Schwarcz, V. (1986) *The Chinese Enlightenment: Intellectuals and the Legacy of the May Fourth Movement of 1919*, Berkeley, CA: University of California Press.

Shapiro, H. (1965) *Race Mixture*, Paris: UNESCO.

Siddle, R. (1997) 'Ainu: Japan's indigenous people', in M. Weiner (ed.) *Japan's Minorities: The Illusion of Homogeneity*, London: Routledge.

Sikora, J. (1988) 'An assessment of one LEA's attempts to promote multicultural education in its secondary schools', unpublished MEd thesis, University of Manchester

Silverman, M. (1992) *Immigration, Race and Nation in Modern France*, Aldershot: Avebury.

Sivanandan, A. (1983) 'Challenging racism: strategies for the '80s', *Race and Class* 25, 2, pp. 1–11.

—— (1985) 'RAT and the degradation of black struggle', *Race and Class* 26, 4, pp. 1–33.

Snowden, F. (1983) *Before Color Prejudice: The Ancient View of Blacks*, Cambridge, MA: Harvard University Press.

Sowell, T. (1981) *Markets and Minorities*, Oxford: Basil Blackwell.

—— (1990) *Preferential Policies: An International Perspective*, New York: William Morrow and Company.

Spivak, G. (1990) 'Gayatri Spivak on the politics of the subaltern', *Socialist Review* 20, 3, pp. 81–97.

Steele, S. (1991) *The Content of Our Character: A New Vision of Race in America*, New York: Harper.

Stonequist, E. (1961) *The Marginal Man: A Study in Personality and Culture*, New York: Russell and Russell.

Taguieff, P-A. (1988) *La Force du préjugé: Essai sur le racisme et ses doubles*, Paris: Editions la Découverte.

—— (1995) *Les Fins de l'antiracisme*, Paris: Editions Michalon.

Tate, N. (1994) 'Off the fence of common culture', *Times Educational Supplement*, 29 July.

Taylor, C. (1992) *Multiculturalism and 'The Politics of Recognition'*, Princeton, NJ: Princeton University Press.

Theodore, A. (1994) *The Invention of the White Race: Volume One: Racial Oppression and Social Control*, London: Verso.

Tinker, H. (1987) *Men Who Overturned Empires: Fighters, Dreamers and Schemers*, Madison, WI: University of Wisconsin Press.

Todorov, T. (1993) *On Human Diversity: Nationalism, Racism, and Exoticism in French Thought*, Cambridge, MA: Harvard University Press.

Tomlinson, S. (1990) *Multi-cultural Education in White Schools*, London: Batsford.

Travis, A. (1999) '2001 Census will put faith in religious beliefs', *The Guardian*, 4 January.

Troyna, B. and Williams, J. (1986) *Racism, Education and the State*, London: Croom Helm.

Trudeau, P. (1971) *Federal Government Response to Book IV of the Royal Commission on Bilingualism*, Ottawa: House of Commons.

Turley, D. (1991) *The Culture of English Antislavery, 1780–1860*, London: Routledge.

Turner, J. (1985) 'Brown into black: changing racial attitudes of Afro-Brazilian university students', in P. Fontaine (ed.) *Race, Class and Power in Brazil*, Los Angeles: Center for Afro-American Studies, University of California, pp. 73–94.

Twitchin, J. and Demuth, C. (1981) *Multi-cultural Education*, London: British Broadcasting Corporation.

United States Code of Federal Regulations (1989) *41 Code of Federal Regulations Chapter 60*, Washington, DC: Office of Federal Contract Compliance Programs, Department of Labor.

Vasconcelos, J. (1997) *The Cosmic Race: A Bilingual Edition*, Baltimore: Johns Hopkins University Press.

Vergès, F. (1996) 'To cure and to free: the Fanonian project of "decolonized psychiatry"', in L. Gordon, T. Sharpley-Whiting and R. White (eds) *Fanon: A Critical Reader*, Oxford: Blackwell, pp. 85–99.

Vieira, R. (1995a) 'Brazil', in Minority Rights Group (eds) *No Longer Invisible: Afro-Latin Americans Today*, London: Minority Rights Publications, pp. 19–46.

—— (1995b) 'Black resistance in Brazil: a matter of necessity', in B. Bowser (ed.) *Racism and Anti-racism in World Perspective*, Thousand Oaks, CA: Sage, pp. 227–240.

Voltaire (1964) *Zadig/L'Ingénu*, Harmondsworth: Penguin.

Wallerstein, I. (1991) 'The ideological tensions of capitalism: universalism versus racism and sexism', in E. Balibar and I. Wallerstein *Race, Nation, Class: Ambiguous Identities*, London: Verso, pp. 29–36.

Warder, M. (1993) 'The politics of culture war', *Vital Speeches of the Day* 59, pp. 653–656.

Ware, V. (1992) *Beyond the Pale: White Women, Racism and History*, London: Verso.

Wazir, B. (1998) 'Dane gets race jibes payout', *The Guardian*, 31 October.

Wellman, D. (1977) *Portraits of White Racism*, Cambridge: Cambridge University Press.

Werbner, P. (1997) 'Essentialising essentialism, essentialising silence: ambivalence and multiplicity in the constructions of racism and ethnicity', in P. Werbner and T. Modood (eds) *Debating Cultural Hybridity: Multi-Cultural Identities and the Politics of Anti-racism*, London: Zed Press, pp. 226–256.

Wiesenthal, S. (1967) *The Murderers Among Us*, New York: McGraw-Hill.

Wieviorka, M. (1997) 'Is it so difficult to be anti-racist?', in P. Werbner and T. Modood (eds) *Debating Cultural Hybridity: Multi-Cultural Identities and the Politics of Anti-racism*, London: Zed Press, pp. 139–153.

Willett, C. (ed.) (1998) *Theorizing Multiculturalism: A Guide to the Current Debate*, Oxford: Blackwell.

Williams, E. (1966) *Capitalism and Slavery*, New York: Capricorn Books.

—— (1970) *From Columbus to Castro: The History of the Caribbean, 1492–1969*, London: Deutsch.

Wintour, P. (1995) 'UK race laws the best, says Howard', *The Guardian*, 25 November.

Wolff, L. (1994) *Inventing Eastern Europe: The Map of Civilization on the Mind of the Enlightenment*, Stanford, CA: Stanford University Press.

Wright, J. (1979) 'Positive image: negative effect', *Issues in Race and Education* 21, pp. 1–3.

X, Malcolm (1987) *Two Speeches by Malcolm X*, New York: Pathfinder.

Young, R. (1995) *Colonial Desire: Hybridity in Theory, Culture, and Race*, London: Routledge.

INDEX

DATE DUE